THAT INVINCIBLE SAMSON

THAT INVINCIBLE SAMSON

The Theme of
Samson Agonistes in World Literature
with Translations of the
Major Analogues

by

WATSON KIRKCONNELL

President Emeritus, Acadia University

UNIVERSITY OF TORONTO PRESS

PREFACE

THIS STUDY of the analogues of *Samson Agonistes* began as a by-product of my larger project on the analogues of *Paradise Lost*,[1] in the course of which I found myself constantly stumbling upon material relevant to Milton's other works as well. It was significant, for example, that the Jacobite Milton-hater, William Lauder, did not confine his charges of plagiarism to *Paradise Lost* but listed a *Samson Agonistes* (1547) by Hieronymus Zieglerus and another *Samson Agonistes* (1604) by Marcus Andreas Jounstus[2] as among the forerunners who were hijacked by the "Plagiarorum Princeps."[3] In more recent times, George Edmundson[4] claimed Vondel's *Samson of Heilige Wraeck* as a manifest and sinfully unacknowledged source of Milton's play, while George W. Whiting[5] has argued for a minor but authentic influence in Francis Quarles's *The Historie of Samson* (1631). A much wider net was cast by F. Michael Krouse in his *Milton's Samson and the Christian Tradition*.[6] His primary interest was in theological commentaries through the centuries but he also listed a large number of Renaissance plays on Samson in Latin, German, French, Spanish, Italian, and Dutch, scarcely any of which had been studied. Kurt Gerlach, in *Der Simsonstoff im deutschen Drama*,[7] cited dozens of analogues, in Latin and in German, ranging from the Middle Ages to the twentieth century but confined in provenance to Germany. Will Tissot's

[1]*The Celestial Cycle* (Toronto, 1952), xxviii, 701.
[2]A misprint for Wunstius. In both of these instances, Lauder tampered with the title by adding an "Agonistes" that was not in the original.
[3]*Delectus Auctorum Sacrorum Miltono Facem Praelucentium* (London, 1753), II, xxviii, xxxvi.
[4]*Milton and Vondel* (London, 1885).
[5]*Milton's Literary Milieu* (Chapel Hill, 1939).
[6]Princeton, 1949.
[7]Berlin, 1929.

Simson und Herkules[8] concentrates on the Baroque Period.
Roy Daniells[9] has now added a new dimension to the field
of poetic analogy by revealing the artistic relationship between
the structure of *Samson Agonistes* and the baroque archi-
tectural idiom of the church of S. Andrea al Quirinale,
erected by Giovanni Lorenzo Bernini (1598–1680).

My purpose in the present volume, as in *The Celestial
Cycle*, is to go back in every instance to primary sources and
to examine all treatments of Milton's theme in all languages
for their intrinsic interest and merit. While a discussion of
source relationships is not entirely omitted, the concern of the
volume is with analogues.

In Part I of the book, five pre-Miltonic works are given,
in whole or in part, for significant comparison with *Samson
Agonistes*. I have translated entire, from Latin and from
Dutch respectively, two plays that are strictly in the Attic
tradition—the *Simson* of Marcus Andreas Wunstius and the
Samson of Heilige Wraeck of Joost van den Vondel. I have
also added, from the Italian, the whole of Giattini's oratorio,
Il Sansone (1638). As of lesser interest, extracts only are
given from the *Samson* of Hieronymus Zieglerus and the
Simson of Theodorus Rhodius.

In the Descriptive Catalogue that follows as Part II will
be found brief comments on the significance of a hundred
or so analogues, both to Miltonists and to the general reader.
Thus any critic who has denounced Milton for his chorus'
unfriendly remarks about women, as represented by Delilah,
will find that their language is cambric tea by comparison
with that of Milton's forerunners, even as far back as Abelard,
Prodromus, Petrus Comestor, Boccaccio, and Lydgate. Inci-
dentally, their words (in Milton) are wholly in character for
the crusty old Danites who have seen their champion betrayed by a woman. It is childish, out of some anachronisti-

[8]Stadtroda, 1932.
[9]*Milton, Mannerism and Baroque* (Toronto, 1963), pp. 209–19.

cally Romantic sympathy for Mary Powell, spitefully to indict Milton on these grounds as a woman-hater. Significant again in most of the plays before 1670 is some basic ulterior purpose beyond mere theatre. There are warnings to Catholics against Protestants and to Protestants against Catholics; there are exhortations to young men to shun the perils of lust and the wiles of loose women; there are morals drawn from the whole range of theological commentary, in which, for example, Samson foreshadows Christ yet is himself a very human sinner who rises through penitence to sainthood and revengeful martyrdom. It would be strange if *Samson Agonistes*, standing in such a tradition, did not carry some overtones of personal, national, or theological significance.

After 1671 there is a rapid shift away from a religious or moral presentation of Samson to one of mere theatrical entertainment. This has obscured from most of the critics of later centuries the tone and tradition of this great drama. Even the roots of the purely dramatic treatment may be found in the Middle Ages, however, interspersed in the dominantly Christian *auto* or mystery play as callithumpian elements of jest and jumping about. Beginning with Perez de Montalván's *El Valiente Nazareno* (1638), this primitive version rises to courtly melodrama and launches a fashion that reaches its climax in Romagnési's *Samson* (1730) and the opera of Lemaire and Saint-Saëns (1877). The nineteenth and twentieth centuries have seen dozens of versions of the old play theme, nearly all of them wholly disregarding any inner drama of the spirit and stressing extrovert aspects of Strength, Beauty, and Sex. Analogues 68 to 107 will reveal something of the variety that playwrights have found possible in the ancient theme. In the interests of brevity, the analysis of all analogues has been left to the Descriptive Catalogue.

One may add, however, that to consider Milton's *Samson Agonistes* against this background of one hundred other writers of all ranks is to conclude soberly that the play must be judged in terms of its own declared purpose, the concepts and knowledge of its maker, and the success of the artistry that forged its verse and its dramatic pattern. Even our crudely egalitarian age cannot explain away the creative imagination of a great spirit in terms of borrowed materials and literary gimmicks, as if every supreme writer were a Madison Avenue huckster of synthetically fabricated propaganda. To this humble classical scholar, at any rate, *Samson Agonistes* is by far the noblest treatment of its theme ever written, approached in literary quality only by Vondel and far more profound than its Dutch predecessor because its drama is inward and spiritual rather than outward and physical and traces progressively the psychological stages by which its hero advances from despair through successive testings to ultimate resolution, faith, and victory. The "middle" that Johnson failed to recognize is now seen as the cumulative structure of a tragedy that may fairly challenge most of the surviving dramas of Athens' greatest period.

WATSON KIRKCONNELL

Acadia University
Wolfville, Nova Scotia

CONTENTS

Part One

ANALOGUES

HIERONYMUS ZIEGLERUS

Samson, Tragoedia Nova
1547
Samson, A New Tragedy*

―❧❧―

Dramatis Personae

Manue, *father of Samson*
Aecara, *mother of Samson*
Samson, *a judge of Israel*
Eleasar, Heber, Joachim, Jacob,
  a messenger, *Israelites*
Agrypnus, Jabis, Micha, *princes*
  of the Philistines
Band of thirty companions
Thamnatus, *father of the bride*

Thamnatis, *bride of Samson*
Philistine army
Delilah
Abra, *a nurse*
Laomor, *a barber*
Philistines, *who capture Samson*
  at Delilah's house
Talion, *a hangman*
Boy

PROLOGUE

I bring you a new tragedy, my friends,
And beg you to attend with gracious ears.
The fable may be very old indeed,
Yet who has gazed upon it hitherto
Rendered in such a fashion? To this theme

---

*Translation by Watson Kirkconnell from the Latin of Zieglerus. The iambic senarius of the original dialogue has been turned into blank verse in English.

Praise has been given that, whate'er it is,
Its ways are fashioned by the will of God.
This I would beg you all to recognize
With just discrimination; base it were
Merely to parrot what was said before.
Most fair it is, however, to re-edit
Well in another form what has been taken
Out of the Bible. For if one should choose
To deal with topics that are secular,
Then let him read the stories that were written
By Terence and by Plautus in their fashion.
But it is fitting that a Christian first
Should learn examples of a moral life
And standards from the Scriptures; thus to drink
The waters of the oracles of God
And know more strictly what His will may be,
While those whose portion is the wandering world
Will follow after all things, foul or fair.
Therefore, I beg you, grant me audience.
All faithful Christians through the world's wide bounds
Now fear the Turks and deem that none have power
To fight against them or to wish to fight:
A thing absurd! As if Almighty God,
No longer mindful of us, should permit
His own to come to ruin. Not at all
Is this the truth, as Israel bears witness,
And not in one case only, whom that God,
One and the Same, has punished grievously
With long captivity and servitude
To other nations and has penalized
With hunger, thirst and pestilence, but never
Permitted them to be exterminated:
Nay rather, He has raised them up again
By the right hand of His power. Before Samson
Became their judge, how much did they endure?

Yet I were mute concerning all the rest.
Did He not justly at the last avenge
His people by the holy strength of Samson?
Although he had been captured, had been blinded,
He in his death destroyed a greater host
Than all that he had slain while still alive—
So that the Philistines might know indeed
The God of Israel, how great He was,
And Who, and how almighty a Defender
Of His own folk. The temple's dread collapse
Is a most certain witness that to foes
God is a peril and no trifling one.
Therefore let saints now living greatly hope
That victory may be given them from heaven
Against the barbarous Turks, our mighty foes,
When it seems good to God, by Whose decree
The destinies of mankind rise and fall.
A proof of this to you is manifest
In Samson's story. As we tell it here,
You in due course will understand what more
The tragedy brings with it. We shall strive
Most earnestly to help you comprehend. . .

ACT ONE

Manoah, his wife, and their friends Eleasar and Heber are all concerned that Samson, the pride and hope of his country, should make a good marriage.

ACT TWO

Samson refuses to marry the Hebrew red-head, a neighbour's daughter, whom they have chosen for him. He insists rather on marrying a beautiful Philistine girl from the town of Thamnat. Samson soliloquizes on the lion he had slain and the honey found in it. The thirty Philistine groomsmen are baffled by his riddle.

A C T   T H R E E

The groomsmen ferret out the answer through his wife. He kills thirty Philistines in order to pay his wager with their garments. When his father-in-law gives the bride to another, Samson declares war on the Philistines, burns their crops, and kills a thousand men at the rock Etam.

A C T   F O U R

Samson soliloquizes over his exploit with the gates of Gaza. Delilah promises the Philistine princes to secure from her lover, Samson, the secret of his strength. She at last succeeds and, while he is sleeping, she has his hair cut off. He is now easily captured. The Philistines, after debating his fate, put out his eyes on the stage. He indulges in a long lament over the iniquity of women and his own weakness.

A C T   F I V E

Scene 1

(*Enter* PRINCES OF THE PHILISTINES)

FIRST PRINCE

> Now we are freed at last from grievous fear;
> We hold our enemy in bonds most sure,
> And all the thanks are due our deity,
> Great Dagon: it is he who has delivered
> Into our hands that Samson who had burned
> The harvests of our fields and struck down many
> With a most mighty hand. But now forsooth
> He has become a jest, even a tale,
> Blind, wretched, and a slave beneath our power.
> Henceforth this festival will be observed,
> Year after year, throughout the entire city
> To our demesne's far bounds. To holy Dagon
> Let men now come and offer up a gift.

SECOND PRINCE

>A public banquet we shall now prepare.
>Let all the temples be bedecked with flowers,
>Let all the floors be carpeted with grass
>And let fresh violets adorn our brows!
>Rejoice, then, lads; rejoice, old men and maidens;
>For this is Dagon's festival; mount up
>Into the temples. Let us chorus there.

THIRD PRINCE

>Ho, there! Bid Samson to this place be brought,
>That he may dance here. You, centurion,
>May have this in your charge. Although the feast
>Delights us and the wine brings equal pleasure,
>The dance of Samson will enhance our joy.
>>(Enter SAMSON)
>He himself comes; bring forth the tuneful pipes;
>Let all of our musicians be at hand.
>The high, exalted judge of Israel
>Is going to dance. His hair is growing back,
>His locks are manifestly thicker now
>And still his hands are moist with recent blood,
>His fierce face threatens crimes, his eyes drip
>>frenzy.
>Now may our gods ward off all cause for fear!
>Let him, centurion, first wet his throat,
>Give him the cup. Drink, Samson! In this fashion
>Accept a glass brimmed high with Gentile wine
>And pour out a libation to our gods.
>Then you will grace our holiday with dancing.

Scene 2

(SAMSON. THE PRINCES. A BOY)

SAMSON

>By all the pleasure I have given you,

Poor blind wretch that I am, I am worn out
In both my feet, and have no eyes to guide me.

PRINCE

You shall gain nothing thus. Dance on, dance on.
Skip in your wonted style, your Hebrew fashion.
Sing, O musicians, to the harp, and play,
And we shall watch a judge of Israel
Dance trippingly. Behold, how well he dances!
Keep on, the measure's good, it pleases us.
Stand aside, yonder, give him room to gambol.
All this is done in honour of our god:
Dagon for this keeps Samson's soul alive.

SAMSON

I beg you, let a poor wretch rest a little.

PRINCE

Rest, then, a while. Your task will soon return.
We, in the meantime, are constrained to drink.
O Princes of Philistia, come hither
And follow me.

SAMSON   Alas, how hot I am!
My limbs are wearied most exceedingly;
Sweat foams upon my flesh and trickles down.
Ho, there, my boy. Take me aside, I pray.
Let me but touch those columns on whose heads
The mighty building holds its ponderous weight.
There would I rest. Do you withdraw some
          distance.
But tell me what the Philistines are doing.

BOY

They eat, they drink, three thousand at one feast.

SAMSON

It is enough, be still. Go far away,
And do not come again till you are called.

(*Exit* Boy)

O Lord, my God, remember me this day,
And give me back the strength that once I had,
So that on impious foes I may take vengeance
And reap a penalty for loss of eyes.
May this strong, lofty habitation fall,
This devil's den, even on me, provided
It also topple on my enemies.
Come, O my soul, let us essay a deed
At which my land's remote posterity
Shall never grieve and never cease to speak.
Behold a monstrous, dark and bloody crime
Inflicted on me by the Philistines
Must be avenged. Wherefore let God vouchsafe
To bless my purpose; without hesitation
I now press on. So let the temple fall,
Let all here perish, hopelessly together
Let men and women die, all who attend.
Now let my soul die with the Philistines!
For death alone can save the innocent.

Scene 3

(*Enter* Boy, *alone*)

Boy

Ah, fearful fate from heaven, this blind man's
    frenzy!
Alas for savage deeds, malign and horrid;
Ah, the sad evil of that mighty fall!
He has thrown down the fane in utter ruin.
Alas, the town's calamity! O Dagon,
See what this sightless man has brought upon you!
All men and boys and women here are dying,
Nor has a soul, save me, escaped the carnage.
Here severed feet and fingers lie apart,

And there an arm, and there a head shorn off
Gapes at the wound it left. The horrid gore
Flows gushing from the body left behind,
And there the bloodless features stare distorted.
A gory wife is mashed up with her husband
And children with their parents mingled lie
With widening signs of slaughter on their
      garments.
Behold the building sinister with death.
The temple is completely overturned,
Its roof has fallen. There remains for us
Only the mighty harvest of our tears.
Hither, come hither, citizens, and bring
Their sad remains. Dust lies on every man.
All has been lost, our glory is extinct,
For here our princes lie, with rubble mixed.
Fear seizes on the city, lest the Jews
Should now oppress us. Those who when alive
Used to defend our state, now lie in death.
Whatever general griefs I have lamented
Are deepened by my own. Calamity
Afflicts each man, and mine is dark to me.
Whatever mighty loss our city lacked
Samson has given us. Behold the temple
Is but a mound of wreckage and of men.
But come, what shall I do? Shall I lament
Our fathers and their wives? The death of youth?
Or shed tears for myself and for my country?
Is this our enemy's captivity?
Is this the vengeance that we sought to take
Upon his crimes—who in his bloody death
Slew more than ever in his living forays?
What shall our future be? What may we look to?
There is no hope of safety in our land.
I shall seek out an exile's hiding place

And run the risk of wounding far away
Rather than gaze on evil here at home.
I shall desert my country, and shall flee.

(*Exit* Boy)

MARCUS ANDREAS WUNSTIUS

Simson, Tragoedia Sacra
1600, 1604
Samson, A Sacred Tragedy*

———✽———

Dramatis Personae

Samson
Eluma, *mother of Samson*
A Hebrew priest
A Philistine lord
A herald

Delilah
A barber
A boy, *as messenger*
Chorus of Hebrew maidens

ACT ONE
(Enter ELUMA, *alone)*

ELUMA

Back to the house from which I came I ply
My plodding steps, a woman old and bent,
And on a staff support my failing members,
Even as a house, battered by frequent winds,

*Translation by Watson Kirkconnell from the Latin of Marcus Andreas Wunstius. The iambic senarius of the original dialogue has been rendered into its historical heir, blank verse, while the lyric measures of the chorus are turned into heroic couplets.

Grows gradually weak with rotting rafters,
Until its melting fabric falls in ruins.
Thus day by day the structure of our body
Weakens and waxes old, little by little,
Until, with all its vigour gone, it lapses
Into a sad old age. I think the sea
Is not harassed with hurricanes as many
As are the evils, of both flesh and spirit,
That beat upon old age from every side.
I should, however, much more patiently
Endure these hardships had not God of late
Torn from me the best part of my poor heart,
My bedmate and the anchor of my life,
Support of my declining years, Manoah,
My spouse for fifty years in concord greater
Than that of turtle-doves. This hope alone
Sustains me now—the prospect of that day,
By frequent prayers and due petitions sought,
When with your ashes in the selfsame urn
My own are mingled and our souls shall meet,
Dear husband, in the vestibules of heaven.
That day must shortly come. Meanwhile, my
     son,
Samson, is furnishing great help and comfort
To soothe my widowhood; he only makes
Me live in less discomfort. In his arms,
My soul as it departs will breathe its last,
Samson will close my eyelids as my eyes
Swim in the mists of death; and he will bury
My body and will join his mother's ashes
To those of his dear father. O my God,
With kind assent preserve to me this helper;
And not to me alone; but to Thy people,
Who, caught beneath the black Philistian
     yoke,

Are paying the due penalties of sin,
Even while they spurn Thy edicts and Thy law.
Moved by paternal grace, receive again
This nation as it turns its face to Thee
In penitence of heart. Proceed, O God,
Through this my son's avenging hand to
      shatter
The haughty spirits of the impious foe!
Him Thou didst destine from before his birth
As saviour and avenger of Thy people.
God comes so kindly to the aid of man
As ever to ordain strength in affliction
And an assured way out of grievous woes.

    My heart remembers—it can ne'er forget—
That day when Phadaël, his great face shining,
His gleaming vesture whiter than the snow,
Flew as a youth from heaven to my home.
With tidings glad he rescued me from grief:
God had had pity on my barren state
And on His people's anguish; He would give
Samson, a son to me and to the nation
A leader all-invincible. The years
Fulfilled all this: What mighty proofs of
      strength
He gave at length! When the first tender down
Of manhood had but barely marked his cheeks,
He walked by chance a hidden forest path
And there destroyed a furious great lion,
With gaping maw and eyes of flame, a monster
Not seen before, and, though unarmed, he
      slew
The savage beast, tearing its jaws apart
With his two hands. He later fastened torches
All flaming to three hundred foxes' tails
And sent them flying through Philistian fields.

The flame spread far and wide, and burned to
    ashes
The ripening harvest. Hence came seeds of
    hate
Implacable. Hence frenzy for revenge
Entered the spirits of our enemies;
By day and night they seek to slay my son
And nothing leave untried; meanwhile the
    hero,
Endued with valour and by heaven armed,
Cares nothing for the enemy's proud strength
And threats and wiles. Alone and lacking arms,
He overthrows and slays them by battalions.
    The stock of Judah, by their foemen's threats
Forced to the deed, surrendered up the man,
Close bound with heavy fetters, to the hands
Of the fierce Philistines. While these rejoiced
And thought that days of evil now were past
And planned strong tortures to destroy their
    foe,
His bonds were swiftly broken by his hands
And fell as useless as a rotten thread.
Seeing by chance the jawbone of an ass
That lay there on the ground, he seized upon it
To assault the thickest of the enemy.
Just as a lion, when its cubs are lost,
Attacks without distinction man and beast,
As each may chance to meet his raging fury,
So Samson with an ass's jaw destroys
A thousand men and drives away the rest
In craven flight. Henceforth, such panic enters
The foemen's hearts that presently they
    tremble,
Even in his absence, at his very name.
    One care, however, mars his mother's heart,

Lest, insolent with his success, he lose
The reverence he owes to the Almighty,
To Whom alone, and from his cradle up,
He has in fashion Nazarite been pledged.
   The more each soul is pleasing unto heaven,
The more it is endued with heavenly favour,
The greater caution, even so, in life
Must be maintained, because the Enemy
Of all our race wages unending battle.
Just as a general in hostile fashion
Lays siege to take a royal citadel,
Laden with wealth, and sleeplessly takes note
Of every chance to wage a winning war
Or weave a hidden plot against its fastness,
So Satan ventures with a thousand wiles,
A thousand arts, a thousand traps of sin,
To ruin pious souls by God's permission.
   O quiet Night, mother of human dreams,
How without ceasing thou hast plagued my
     heart
With mournful phantoms. That thy words are
     vain
And full of lies, I pray today, and trust
That rumour brings me false discourse from
     thee.
   But Thou, O heavenly Father, earth's true
     Judge,
Within Whose hand the hearts of men abide,
If matchless might has armed my Samson's
     body,
Permit Thy holy grace to arm his soul.
   But lo, God's herald, grey and venerable,
Who has been wont to soothe my griefs with
     words
Of heavenly peace, comes hither with slow
     step,

He whose discourses have to me been sweeter
Than honey and the honeycomb, yea, better
Than all the riches of the Hindoos' realm.
            (*Enter* PRIEST)

PRIEST

Illustrious ornament of holy women,
Your face is witness that you are tormented
By some new sorrow. Speak then and commit
        it
To my tried confidence, that by my counsel
Or some consoling word your cankered grief
May be alleviated or removed.
For this end, to the limit of my powers
I shall strive carefully. The hapless man
Who broods on hidden woe and feeds in
        silence
Upon his thoughts, unequal at the last
Lies down beneath the burden of his grief.
Like someone shipwrecked in a raging sea,
He still is driven by the cruel waves
Hither and thither. If he puts his trust
In his own strength and heedless fails to grasp
The plank that meets him, after lengthy
        struggles
He sinks in sheer exhaustion to the depths.

ELUMA

Old man, the reverend interpreter
Of heaven's laws, are you astonished still
That I am quite dissolved in endless tears,
I, whom so many dire calamities,
So many evils, public and my own,
Afflict with fear? Now and from childhood up
No day or night has lacked its cloud of cares;

And while old age is dragged in sorrow out,
Ills keep increasing in my wretchedness.
If sleep, a seldom guest, should close my eyes,
My mind is tortured still with mournful
    dreams,
Presaging new affliction. When, alas,
Will God cut short my hated life's delay
And to my many ills ordain an end?

PRIEST

Blind fortune rules us not, nor aimless chance.
Our life's design is in the hand of God.
Whatever mishap comes, bears His consent
Who rules all things. No shadow of disaster
Can come to any man beyond the will
And protocol of heaven. God is our father
And we should all obey a father's laws.

ELUMA

If God attends us with a father's heart,
Why does He load us with calamities?

PRIEST

Those whom He loves, He chastens. 'Tis the
    way
That even human fathers tend their children.
A bridle must restrain the impulses
Of the lascivious. The human mind,
Elated by good fortune, rushes headlong
Into all sorts of crime. What recent care
Has now entrapped you in anxiety?

ELUMA

It has been spread abroad by common rumour
That this my son, forgetful of his office
And of the laws the Almighty has laid down,
Begins to give himself to wantonness,

To wine and wayward lust. If this be true,
How far away, think you, the ruin stands
Of our whole nation, when its judge is
          plunged
Into such sin's defilement? Frequently
Subjects atone for misdeeds of their rulers.
    Last night, as I kept ceaselessly revolving
This thing within my heart, weary with care,
I stooped to languid sleep and closed my eyes.
    Behold a young man stood before my face,
The angel Phadaël sent down from heaven.
Not as before, with shining face and dress,
When he foretold the coming of my son;
But manifesting grief in garb and voice,
In face and gestures, he appeared to speak:
    "The cares, Eluma, that distress and rack
          you
Are not an empty threat; for Samson rages,
Caught in the fetters of infernal guile,
And has forgot the spirit of his God;
Piety cast aside, with careless mind
He piles up sin on sin and so presents
Jehovah's name as a foul laughing stock
For Philistines to gape at. What could be
More terrible than this? God's holy hand
Is therefore armed for heavy punishment.
Unless he now retreats and mends the manners
Of such an impious life while time remains
And while God's door of grace stands open
          still,
Then Samson's day is done. He will provide
A dreadful sport to all his enemies
In a most grievous death. He who affronts
The Deity shall not live on unscathed."
    Thus spoke the youth and vanished in thin air.

I woke at once from sleep, my limbs a-tremble;
Cold sweat flowed down my body, tears made
    wet
My mournful cheeks, the while my trembling
    breast
Quaked with fresh fear. I turn now here, now
    there,
While in my anxious mind I still reflect
On God's dread warning. Also I pursue
The matter higher yet and seek protection
From the impending evil. Yet I fail
To find right counsel in my misery;
And so the harvest of my sorrows grows
With silent pain, and cares are fed on cares.

PRIEST

No mortal lot is blest in every way:
Gall's flavour, even mixed with honey, steals
Its grace of sweetness. Even so, the parents
Who after years of prayer for progeny
Gain them at last, in new anxiety
Are now tormented by a thousand cares.
    Nature, and God its author, surely warn you
That deep solicitude for Samson's fate
Befits his mother; but maternal worry
Is not enough to make a child devout;
Samson must now be warned, be wisely
    blamed,
Be frightened by God's wrath and hell's grim
    fire.
Then when our toil, bereft of heavenly aid,
Has vanished down the wind, we must invoke
The aid of God, who holds within His hand
The hearts of all men, young and old alike.
    Yet it may be, mankind's accustomed gossip
Today has brought this lying tale abroad,

Gnawing with envious tooth the reputation
Of one yet innocent. Nor can one trust
All of one's dreams. For often deep-set care
Breeds in the mind unquiet sleep at night.
    I see a cohort of the enemy
Approach in arms. What do they purpose here?
Let's go within: without their hostile witness
I would converse upon this matter further.

(*Exeunt* PRIEST *and* ELUMA; *enter* PHILISTINE PRINCE
and SOLDIERS)

PRINCE

Comrades in arms, the news is now that Samson,
The foeman, shame and ruin of our people,
Has entered Gaza. Auspices are good
And augurs tell us that the entrails show
A happy outcome for our enterprise.
Dagon at last, the greatest of the gods,
Has looked on us with gracious countenance.
Our part is now with bravery to follow
The admonitions of the blessed gods
While our own injuries cry out for vengeance.
Sluggish delay can only bring us loss.
How should we fear the conquering strength of one
Who now lies vanquished in a whore's embrace?
Soft love has always made a brave man weak
And clouds the sunlight of a healthy mind
Till he no longer knows the prudent way.
So long as Samson led a blameless life,
He stood beneath the shelter of some god
Who still endowed him with a dauntless hand.
But now base love has laid him under siege;
Foul lust displaces former purity;
And all of heaven's favour flees away.
The gods renounce all aid to sinful men.
May Samson pay the penalty condign

For all his cruelty thus far committed
And may the glory of our victory
Wipe out the earlier blot of our disgrace!
We hold him shut within the city ramparts,
Captive with bronze more strong than chains of iron,
All through the wiles of a licentious woman.
While night drives off the day, let us encompass
The city and hem round each single gate
In silence with a mighty force of arms.
Suspecting nothing, he will promptly fall
Into the power of his enemies.
With compact ranks we'll take him unawares
And then torment our captive with slow death
And tortures infinite. If he resist
And will not yield to us alive, the field
Will give his body, into gobbets cut,
As scattered food to birds and ravening beasts.
If, in this play, your votes agree with mine,
Brandish your spears in token of assent:
And follow me, your chief, through every hazard.

(*Exeunt*)

CHORUS OF HEBREW MAIDENS

O listless brother of cold death, that flies
On shadowy wings by night across the skies,
Creeping unseen to ply a drowsy potion,
Robbing the body of its wonted motion,
Breathing with friendly breath upon the sight
To shut its portals from the hated light:
Wherefore, O Sleep, did the Great Architect
Create thee first? Was it by rest to effect,
In sweet repose that counteracts life's moil,
Refreshment of our bodies after toil,
And resurrect the strength that will not stay
In bodies broken by the tasks of day?
Why then the breasts of men who slumbering lie

Dost thou with dreams torment and terrify?
   With a harsh creditor this merchant strives
And in his empty till no coin survives.
Where'er he walks, he casts his eyes about,
Fearing a dunning voice's ruthless shout.
He seeks the empty home he left before,
Then blenches at all knockings on the door;
And the instructed servant still denies
His presence in the home in which he lies.
Then, being caught, he weaves a wistful wraith
Of many words, devoid of all good faith,
And fashions long delays upon delays.
As soon, O Sleep, as he has walked thy ways,
Thou art at hand to show him bounteous wealth.
Tricked by thy semblance into solvent health,
He digs out tawny treasure from the ground
And gapes rejoicing at the gold he's found.
But when, O Sleep, thou dost depart again,
These joys go too; to air the gold flits vain;
Old cares return, for penury to vouch:
He lies a poor man on an empty couch.
   Another man with empty belly sleeps:
And presently a lordly table heaps
A noble banquet high before his face.
Deluded by the semblance of its grace,
He thinks that he is gorging on its store;
Then wakes, and famine seizes him once more.
   Thou has set deadly foes in this man's sight,
Dismaying him with a terrific fight.
   To one thou givest monsters of dread size
And herds of savage beasts before his eyes.
   One man thou castest in the sea's vast waves
And one in conflagrations roasts and raves;
After the hideous visions disappear,
Cold sweat flows from his limbs made wet with fear.

One man, thrown headlong from a lofty tower,
Wakes while he falls, and blesses the glad hour,
Full of thanksgiving, at the end of dread,
To lie uninjured on his downy bed.
   But who, O Sleep, could count the forms past
      number
Thou offerest to mortals while they slumber?
Nor are these always empty and deceiving;
Sometimes that dreams were true and worth believing
Was proved in deeds thereafter. I recall
Examples that our fathers saw befall.
   Jacob, the twelve tribes' father, while he fled
The wrath his brother poured upon his head,
Under the open sky lay down to sleep.
He saw a mighty staircase, high and steep,
Whose topmost step touched heaven's celestial mirth,
Whose lowest rested on the dreary earth;
On this he saw the angel hosts unending
Mounting to heaven and to earth descending.
   This staircase is a figure of the Christ
Who will, in time to come, be sacrificed;
This true Messiah, who is God, the Son
Of God above; when centuries have run
Their course ordained, He will become a man,
Born of a virgin's womb by God's great plan.
With His own blood He'll wash away the stain
Of all our sins and open for us plain
A pathway to the stars. O happy those
To whom Himself our God will then disclose!
   Likewise for Joseph did a vision plumb
The secret evidence of days to come,
When he beheld the stars and sun and moon
Pay honour to him; by a kindred boon,
Eleven sheaves bowed down before his own;
Guided by God, he made the meaning known.

And Pharaoh's wondrous dreams of course foretold
Events thereafter in the days of old.
   Alas, I fear: too much, alas, I fear
The mother, with a heart foreseeing, here
Knows the sad danger that her son may earn.
   Do Thou, O God, on Whom all hinges turn,
Look down, we pray, with fatherly eyes benign,
Upon our fortunes that are truly Thine.

ACT TWO

(Enter SAMSON, *carrying the gates of Gaza)*

SAMSON

   Whenever rosy dawn, as it has driven
The night away, has sown its glorious light
High in the gleaming sky, my agèd mother,
Accompanied by virgins in chaste chorus,
Is wont to offer up her holy prayers
Here in this place. But see, how fortunate,
She herself comes to meet me as I walk.
   Dear Mother, daughters of great Abraham,
The dawn with shining torch has driven off
The shadows, and with rosy face announces
That day is come. If any cloud of grief
Has plagued your bosoms, may it now depart,
Displaced by the glad tidings that I tell
Of deeds that this right hand has now achieved.

ELUMA

   A long disease can have no sudden cure,
Except by sudden death. But tell me now,
Into what fitting fate I bear my breast,
Though it may be the hazard of misfortune.

SAMSON

   How far superior to wicked plots
True strength may be, and how its comrade valour

May tower about wiles, this night has taught,
Made famous by a novel victory.
For when the enemy had deemed me caught,
Hemmed in by walls, with no escape remaining,
Because the gates were closed, when blackest night
Had seized the central highway of the sky,
In one fierce tug I tore from Gaza's walls
These gates and gateposts with their bars and locks.
With these as weapons, I forthwith attacked
The serried columns of the enemy
And put to rout a great part of their host;
Darkness and trembling flight has saved a few.
This door on my left arm became a shield;
My right hand held this sword; as some fierce lion
Assails the gentle flock with bloody maw
And rages in his slaughter, so raged I.
Signs of the recent fight are still apparent
And gore is dripping from the foeman's gate.
    Dear Mother, it seemed good to announce this joy
To you, whose spirit is still gnawed upon
By the vexatious teeth of barren care.
Towards tearing off the chains of slavery
In whose harsh bondage we are long restrained
This present slaughter marks a great step forward.

ELUMA

My son, I do indeed congratulate
You and our nation on this victory
Gained by your hand over our ancient foes.
But fear has settled in my inmost fibres;
Alas, a fear presaging utter evil
Has blocked off every road to happiness.

SAMSON

Grief often walks indeed with palsied age;
But why does such great sorrow rule your mind,
Forbidding you to join in public triumph?

ELUMA

'Tis you yourself, my son, who cause my tears
And all the sighs that rack my heart with care,
Alas, how many sleepless nights I pass,
Uncertain of your safety at all times!

SAMSON

Mother, you nourish empty cares and fears.
Remember the long record of your life:
Our fortunes never stood in better state.

ELUMA

In bitter lamentation was I born,
In it have lived, and every step of life
Has brought me evil. But my mind foresees
A greater evil yet than aught of these.
For not without due penalty shall be
The sins you cherish. God as avenger follows
The evildoer's path. Alas, my son,
One does not vanquish enemies alone
By force of arms; and strength of body merits
But little praise; while great the victory
If you subdue the passions of your heart.
The measure of your service to the state
In bloody conquest is the measure too
Of popular occasions for dread crime.
By the authority of gifted men
Their well-known vices spread among the masses
And so they harm the flock by their example.

SAMSON

Mother, if ill report concerning me
Has reached your ears, you know how commonly
Men love to gnaw upon the reputation
Of blameless mortals with a livid tooth.
You know with what great labour I'm beset.
If, then, the bridle of my life is slackened,
It is to seek a little breathing space.

Even hard-tempered steel can still be broken
Without some respite for its metal sinews.
Toil always needs an interval of rest.

ELUMA

That which to you is trifling relaxation
Will bring deep sighs to me, and you as well.
A hasty pleasure brings enduring sorrow.
These are not trifles: lechery, forsooth,
And drunken fornication, when your vows
To God are broken in forgetfulness
And a proud spirit swells in confidence:
These will bring down the certain wrath of God.

SAMSON

Success in all my doings has been constant;
This speaks of heaven's favour, not its anger.

ELUMA

God does not hasten headlong into wrath
Though punishment be due, but tarries long
In retribution; patient He looks down
And hopes that by repentance you may soon
Regain the path and change your impious ways
Into devotion and due piety.
When this is vain, at length His flaming fury
Rages against you and His ear is deaf
To sudden prayers. But for a space of time
He like a father weighs His high indulgence
Against poor hostile man's atrocities.

SAMSON

Mother, no frenzy has bewitched my soul;
Some instinct sent from heaven draws me on.
Against our public enemies, all things
Are still permissible. Rid, then, your soul
Of these vain cares. Leave all for me to do.

My understanding of my sacred duty
Is quite enough for me. But to fulfil
A solemn vow after my victory
I am withdrawing to the lofty ridge
Of yonder mountain to set up these gates
As a memorial for men to come.
Farewell, my Mother, be assured that life
Is ever ordered by the hand of God.

(Exit SAMSON)

CHORUS

Dear sisters, wreathe with particoloured flowers
Your fragrant tresses, for this day's bright hours
Come to be hymned aloud with chorus glad
And jubilation for the grace we've had.
The favour of the Almighty, long withholden,
Once more has blessed us with a triumph golden.
Freedom once more lifts up its battered head
From the low ground on which it lay as dead.
Through Samson's conquering arm, our foemen's
        hearts
Are numb with fear, their fortitude departs.
Eternal glory has the victor gained,
And we know jubilation unrestrained.
Thus far, new youth to Samson has been given;
He flourishes in valour sent from heaven;
New triumph from his hand we now have seen
To keep the sons of Isaac fresh and green.

Flowers are the grace of maiden modesty
And flowers the signs of festal joy can be.
Ho, then, and garland, for the day's renown,
Your maiden tresses with a floral crown.
A flower is fair to see, and fragrant too,
But ah, too fleeting in our human view!
The bud that opened with the morning star
I have seen carried off by Hesper's car.

In its brief doom, the flower marks, alas,
The treacherous shifts through which we mortals pass!
   Fortune, in one brief moment, in estate
Has raised the humblest and brought down the great.
The simple flower is a material thing;
Up from its mother, earth, behold it spring;
It creeps along the ground; it draws its food
Up from the fields, and when its days conclude,
Back to earth's bosom it returns again.
And even so, all of the sons of men
Are worms of earth, the offspring of the sod;
Maternal Earth has fed us from her clod;
And when we die, as all have died before,
She takes us deep into herself once more.

   The reaper, with his crescent sickle keen,
Harvests bright flowers with the grasses green,
Disdaining every argument of worth,
Of perfume and of beauty upon earth.
And so the judge and ruler of all breath,
Who wields the threatening scimitar of death,
Will reap without distinction every life
That falls, or soon or late, beneath his knife.

   Although the Winter with its frigid stroke
May strip the meadow of its graceful cloak;
Though flowers may wither and their stalks be stubble;
Yet after all this penury of trouble
The gentle breezes of the Spring come back,
And gracious sunshine marks the Zodiac,
Till the glad visage of the reborn earth
Grows in the greening sward to floral birth.

   So each of us, by Death's hand overcome,
Shall find our place within the dusty tomb,
And in sweet sleep shall duly take our rest
Like a small child upon its mother's breast;
Till on the final Resurrection Day

Almighty God's clear voice we all obey
And rise again with radiant aureoles
To share a blessed life with ransomed souls.
    And then our bodies, freed of earth's foul blight,
Shall shine in glory like the sun's pure light,
Sharing the brightness of the angel host.
No grief is there, nor sorrow; fear is lost;
There is no harm, nor sickness, nor decay,
But only holy joys that last for aye.

ACT THREE

(*Enter* DELILAH *and* A MAIDSERVANT)

DELILAH

Decked charmingly enough, I'll venture out.
My maid, inspect me now from head to foot;
Tell me if this bright fillet, gay with gold,
Aptly adorns my head with charm and grace;
If ceruse decks my face with snowy hues
That else my ruddy cheeks would violate;
And if my collar, made of finest linen,
Is broad enough and bored expertly through
So that its little chain hangs stiff with gold.
Advise me carefully if aught's neglected;
For if my beauty ever needed care,
It must be seen to now most carefully.
I, a soft huntress, set my readied nets
To snare a much-sought beast; yes, I prepare
With a fair harlot's wiles to breach the strength
Of Samson, to all men invincible.
    I speak, a woman by experience taught.
There is no man alive with mind so cautious
And with a spirit so unconquerable
That wiles of woman cannot take him in.
But see, the prey is entering my net.

(*Enter* SAMSON)

SAMSON

> O day with golden rays upon me risen,
> Offering yourself a vision to mine eyes,
> My star, my darling, my delight, my soul!
> Bereft of you, no day can be endured.
> And without you, alas, I sadly pass
> A thousand sleepless nights in living one.
> Delilah, let me know your sweet embrace
> And I shall plant a thousand ardent kisses
> Upon your lovely cheeks. Why do you turn
> Your face away? And why repel my hands?

DELILAH

> Your sweet voice hides deceit and wiles of heart.
> O faithless man, consider now if you
> Have not made sport enough of one poor woman.

SAMSON

> If this my heart does not adore you more
> Than these my eyes, may I be pledged to lose
> My eyes and all their joy in gracious light.

DELILAH

> High-sounding words are different from deeds.

SAMSON

> Whatever wealth the universe contains
> Is dross to me compared to you alone.

DELILAH

> Since you, false man, would flatter me with words,
> Be banished, prithee, from my side forever.
> Alas, for the too trustful race of girls
> Who in the sequel must regret and grieve
> And be ashamed for what their faith has granted!

SAMSON

> What crime against you have I now committed
> Worthy of being meted such constraint?

DELILAH

    Love is not genuine that lies in words
    And the brief pleasure of the body's deeds,
    But only that which issues from the heart.
    Could you be mine? And I yours, after this?
    You who conceal the thing you call your heart
    Deep in the silent caverns of your breast
    And cleverly deceive an innocent
    And trusting maid. How many times have you,
    When asked with tears and prayers whence came your
        strength,
    Revealed the truth to me? I have been mocked;
    My prayers have always failed; your empty words
    Have laughed at me again and yet again.
    Thus am I loved. Nay, leave my hands alone.

SAMSON

    Why are you eager to seek out this secret?

DELILAH

    Why would it hurt to tell me what I ask?

SAMSON

    Secrets are safe to keep, a risk to tell.

DELILAH

    Be sure you never will persuade me more
    To join you in the sharing of true love
    Since you conceal the secrets of your breast.
    Did you before consider me disloyal
    When I had yielded you myself unstinted?
    My loyalty is suspect now—and you
    Can do without my love and my embraces.
    You have displayed yourself a friend in words
    But hide a faithless passion in your heart.
    Such is your nature, so, farewell. Go, seek
    Some other victim to deceive with cunning.
    I have already had my fill of words.
            (*She walks away*)

SAMSON

> Now she is gone, raging with fearful wrath.
> As soft wax flows at the approach of fire,
> My heart is melting in the flames of love.
> To it I must surrender. Come, Delilah!
> You conquer. Pray come back. But promise me,
> By all things holy, all fidelities,
> The laws of our true love and God Himself,
> That you will never breathe to mortal ear
> The secret that I give you from my heart.

DELILAH

> By all things holy, all fidelities,
> The laws of our true love, the gods themselves,
> I swear I shall be mute as any stone.

SAMSON

> My trembling mind, presaging some great evil,
> Dreads to reveal this fact in any fashion.
> But cruel love, set in my inmost marrow,
> Compels my will and drives away all fear.
> Turn hither then your gentle eyes, that you
> May mark the locks that hang down to my shoulders.
> In them my fate is set. Not without counsel
> Of God himself, from my first swaddling clothes
> Scissors and razor have not touched my head.
> My strength has here its seat. While this is fresh,
> The vigour of my frame is unabated;
> But if it be cut off, my strength departs.
> The matter is sufficiently explained
> To you in these few words—alas, I fear,
> Too much explained. Behold to what great length
> My yearning for your love has drawn me on.
> Up to my present age I've kept my secret,
> But now I pour it out into your bosom.

DELILAH

> Unless you lie, you are restored to favour.

How easily the minds of girls are swayed
And then swayed back again. Enter my home:
I'll follow you and love you in a moment.
           (SAMSON *enters the house*)
The job is done. The beast is in my net.
The promised gold's as good as in my hand.
Do you, my maid, summon a barber swiftly
That he in silence from the sleeping man
May shave away the hair. Then hasten on
To the Philistian leader, bid him come
With an armed force as promptly as may be.
Let him know Samson has at last been conquered
By my own wiles and has declared to me
The inmost secrets of his silly heart,
Betraying thus his safety and his strength.
After our love, I'll lull him off to sleep,
Reclined upon my breast, his head made drowsy
And doomed to suffer by my blandishments.
Let your first mention be my promised price;
For so it was agreed. Shame is for sale;
And loyalty's for sale; truth, and the gods,
All are for sale for money. At this time,
Nothing is sacred beyond gold. To vanquish
The minds of mighty men renowned for wisdom,
Throughout the whole wide circuit of the world
Naught is more potent than a woman's wiles.
           (*Exit* DELILAH)
CHORUS
A stupor that infatuates the mind,
Deep drowned in base delights, with shadows blind,
Urges it on, with loosened reins of terror,
In a wild runaway of headlong error.
A dreadful penalty, swift footed, thrusts
Inexorably after impure lusts.
God's mind is chaste; with enmity austere
He smites the sinful life in mid-career.

Lust doomed the entire world in days of old
When rains and seas and flooding rivers rolled
Above the mountain summits everywhere
And no earth showed. Preserving by His care
Eight sole survivors, God in sudden wrath,
Spared neither man nor creature in His path.
A spirit sent from heaven showered down
On the foul citizens of Sodom-town
Fierce fires of sulphur. Thence a noxious smoke
Still wafts its evil stench to greet our folk.
How many men among our fathers born
Did Vengeance from on high bestrew in scorn
Through the vast desert, terribly to prove
The penalties that wait on wayward love!
　　The human body is the home ordained
For a celestial spirit. Lust unfeigned
Drives out this guest, installing in its place
A hundred hellish tempests of disgrace.
Coveys of guardian angels still desert
Souls that are sinful; from contagious hurt
They fly, as innocent white doves might seek
To shun a roof made foul by smoky reek.
Do we not know that at the Judgment Day
Our risen bodies shall, if pure, display
Celestial glory, while some filthy fashion
Will mar the lives made foul by wicked passion?
Prayer from chaste hearts its path to heaven cleaves;
God calmly hears and graciously receives.
But if your heart's besieged with madding love,
In vain appeal to heaven your lips will move;
No matter who you are, how eloquent,
Your Heavenly Father grants you no assent.
　　But you will count the ocean's waterdrops
And all the stars that light heaven's boundless copse
Ere you can count the evils, dark as dust,

That Venus brings, the mother of foul lust.
  Alas, I pray, may that be vanity
Which Samson's evil life suggests to me.
If it be true, the Israelites' proud fate
Is doomed indeed, has perished without date.
  Stirred up by God's command and armed by heaven,
He as the saviour of our folk was given.
Alas, alas for grief! Our lot we rue
If Samson's evil actions should be true.
  But you, O Rumour, envious of the good,
Gladly would you as false be understood.
In a too willing heart too soon received,
Whatever is most dreaded is believed.
  Yet, sisters dear, only one cure remains
For all these evils that our anguish feigns—
That upon bended knee, with outstretched hands
And heart submissive, we make meek demands,
Joining together in imploring aid
From God the merciful, our Shield and Shade.
                    (*Enter* BARBER)
BARBER
  My heart beats, and my mind is all aghast;
My legs are trembling; for an image grim
Of death most miserable assails my sight
While I prepare to touch the giant's head
With scissors and with razor and shave off
The mighty Samson's locks of destiny.
Although the awful man is plunged in sleep,
I startle at his snores, his stertorous breathing.
But if he were to rouse, what recompense
Would then be visited upon my labours!
He'd seize me in one hand, tear me apart,
As lions wild bedabble their great paws
In the swift slaughter of a trembling lamb.
But since my deed begets eternal glory,

It calls for a stout heart, a steady hand.
I therefore shall attack. Almighty Dagon,
To whom among the gods I trust myself,
Help thou my venture! Let the task be brief!
And you, cohort of soldiers, be on hand
To clinch the sequel when the hair's been shorn.

SAMSON

Where am I? What is this? And do these fleas
Again disturb my sleep? They once again
Have duly tied my hands behind my back
With rotten ropes; untaught by risk and rout,
They do not dread my sleep nor Samson's shadow.
How now! Alas, the strength that once I knew
Has left my limbs. Hard knots restrain my hands.
I perish through the cunning of a woman:
I see my shorn-off hair upon the floor.
    Spare me, alas! Ah, do not thus gouge out
My eyeballs with your knives! Spare me, alas!
Or since a life bereft of precious light
Is worse than death itself, I pray you slay me!
Slay now a man who in so many ways
Has done you harm! O woman, you inventor
Of treacherous evil, crime unspeakable,
Does this reward befit our mutual love?

PHILISTINE SATRAP

Let him have neither wish! Let him live on,
And live unhappy not in one way only.
Bereft of rest and light, let him wear out
His life as a dull helot at the mill.
This fellow boasts himself invincible.
The mortar of the mill will give him work.
Confine his great neck with a brazen chain
And bind behind his back his mighty hands,
Bloody so often with our people's murder;

Then drag him off to prison. It is fitting
That madness in the dog should thus be broken.

SAMSON

O Father of the universe, to whom
Except to Thee shall I, in anguish set,
Direct the darkened sockets of mine eyes?
Thou seest with how dread a weight of ills
I am oppressed. With wheel how changeable
Dost Thou, O God, alter the fates of mortals!
Only an hour since, in all respects
Most happy, blest, unconquerable in strength,
I now, in sudden lapse, have fallen on ill.
Bereft of eyes, with torn and livid cheeks,
Helpless in chains, a mockery to my foes,
I am thrust deep in nameless slavery
And to this woe no day assigns an end
Except the end of long-awaited death.
What day? Alas, no more, no more will Day
In this my life dawn on my misery.
I am o'erwhelmed in Night's eternal darkness.
    With conscience as my witness, I confess
That I myself, myself alone am cause
Of this unspeakable calamity.
Thou in compassion on Thy chosen people
Hadst destined me a judge and hallowed me
By pledges Nazarite to serve Thyself;
And strength Thou gavest me past mortal limits
And blessed my efforts with untold success.
While I still worshipped Thee and my pure mind
Was faithful, I obeyed Thy holy laws.
But having known fair winds of happiness,
I laid aside my reverence for God;
Puffed up in spirit, blind, devoid of sense,
I rushed into whatever crime my thoughts
Insanely urged, thinking permissible

Whatever I might wish. One must confess
I lacked true sight and so drank shamelessly
The flames of love. Now I must lose my eyes.
The penalty befits my just deserts.

(*Exeunt omnes*)

ACT FOUR

(*Enter* PHILISTINE SATRAP *and* OTHER CITIZENS OF GAZA)

SATRAP

Having removed our helmets and put on
Laurel in victors' wreaths, we celebrate
This day a feast to the most mighty Dagon,
By whose assistance, after many toils,
Our fortunes have attained a healthy state.
Forgetful of his anger, kind in spirit,
Dagon at last has had regard for us.

That Hebrew man, that thunderbolt of strength,
Samson, who raged in slaughtering our men
Like a fierce lion among gentle lambs,
At last lies low; the Hebrew nation, too,
Lies prostrate with him. Can he hope to rise?
Robbed of his strength and eyes, a prisoner,
A slave with slaves, locked up in Gaza's mill?
To fetter him was long beyond our power;
We must ascribe the credit to our god.
Therefore on Dagon's sacred altar-stone
A victim shall be slain; and let the priest,
Deriving hope of valid prayers from thence,
Duly commend our people to our god.

Forthwith we shall indulge in games and feasts
In Dagon's honour, greatest of the gods.
Do you, O herald, loudly cry this order
To all the multitude assembled here,
So that with thankful heart and mind devout
They may crowd hither to this festival.

HERALD

>Ho! Whosoever hears me, let him hush
>And give attentive hearing to the orders
>Of the great lord. Our nation long has suffered
>From mighty perils and has been laid low
>By many slaughters and calamities.
>I think that no one present does not know it.
>The anger of the gods, roused by our sins,
>Ordained these punishments—Dagon himself
>Was first among them, for we had neglected
>The worship due his altars; he permitted
>Our scourging with the pain of all these evils.
>
>(*Exit* SATRAP *and* HERALD)

CHORUS OF HEBREW MAIDENS

>The scourger of the Hebrew folk is gone
>To worship his false god with joy anon;
>In festive ceremony see him go
>To praise our true Jehovah's deadly foe.
>
>How mad those minds by whom the rottenness
>Of wood or lifeless stone is deemed to bless,
>By whom the lumpish likeness of a man
>Is sought out as a god, for boon or ban!
>
>What error of idolatry has glazed
>Your stupid eyes? Can you not see, amazed
>(Yet what can blind men see, in darkness drowned,
>On whom the light of heaven has truly frowned?)
>How still their bodies stand, with fossil feet?
>Their arms how nerveless, lacking vital heat?
>There is no power of seeing in their eyes,
>No power of speaking in their larynx lies,
>No power of hearing in their marble ears.
>Surely you see what stuff its heart appears,
>What substance forms the idol's lungs and brain?
>Mere stone or lumber or a mass inane
>Of melted metal. Can mere lumber then

Or solid stone or metal cast by men
Be capable of hearing human prayers?
Can wood or stone or metal ease our cares?
O maniac minds of men! The gods you trust
Cannot defend themselves from worms or dust
Or moths or flames or billows or decay—
Are you not shamed to turn to such as they?
　　Open your eyes and be aware at last
Of the true God, invisible though vast,
Whose holy nature by His acts is given.
Come, lift aloft your stubborn eyes to heaven!
Does not the sun, with shining lamp, cast forth
His glory on all lands, to south or north,
Reviving all things with his living heat,
Striding to reap the year with tireless feet?
Does not his silent voice to all confess
His great Creator's boundless skilfulness?
Do you not see, this, too, the moon reveals,
Borne through the silent sky on silver wheels,
Presiding over shadowy night austere
And marking off in months the marching year?
The other stars bear witness to the same.
With their due courses in the heavenly frame,
Whether their paths in changeless form endure
Or walk in wandering ways, oblique but sure.
What props the clouds suspended in the sky
Where their stupendous weights in glory lie?—
Only Jehovah's everlasting might.
Behold the swelling sea excel in height
The lowly shingle of the humble shore.
Who holds the Black Sea on its own wet floor
And bids it spare the land? The voice is God's.
He holds the earth unshaken in its clods.
What keeps the shore from toppling in the sea?
Only the right hand of the Deity.
Why pause on details? Not a thing forgetting

That the sun sees in rising and in setting—
All, as with outstretched fingers, point and bring
Their praise to God, their Author and their King.
  O maniac minds of men! Can stone or clay,
Or lifeless trunks, as dead and dumb as they,
Blind, deaf and bloodless in their infamies,
Supply the slightest part of aught of these?
  O God, great Judge above the universe,
We venerate Thy godhead. Though perverse
We bear Thy penalties, yet through our prayers
Madness may smite our proud foes unawares.
We trust Thee therefore with enduring hope,
Knowing Thy heart finds anger in its scope
At a vile mixture of insensate crimes.
Not less we trust Thy love in mercy chimes
To lamentations of the penitent,
Whose knees, in seeking grace, to Thee are bent
In faithful prayer as to a Father kind
Whose goodness is to mercy still inclined.
We know that all who come in shame and grief
And for repented sinning seek relief
Are called by Thy kind voice to springs to go
That ever with Thy goodness bubbling flow.
  In all these storms of deadly circumstance,
One source of help alone greets our mischance:
When anger has raged out its gale of pain,
Our Father's breeze of love will blow again.
When the proud hour of our foes has passed
The billows of the sea will sink at last,
And, with all favourable breezes armed,
The vessel of our state will move unharmed.
Meanwhile, kind Father, give our shoulders strength
To bear our foemen's scorn to any length.
  But whither now is Samson being led,
Bound with great chains, more miserably bestèd
Than anyone alive, ringed by the noise

Of a tormenting crowd of mocking boys?
Let us depart. Chaste maidens must not be
Close to the stain of impious company.
(*Exit* CHORUS. *Enter* SAMSON)

SAMSON

Alas, my life, more bitter far than death!
Where am I dragged? To what dread punishment?
O God, ordain an end to my fierce torments;
Break off at last the lingering light of day!
But why of day? Nay, rather, of this night,
Most terrible and monstrous doom of all!
O Father, I confess this punishment,
Inflicted on me here from heaven by Thee,
Is less than I deserve. My proper place
Would be among the burning fires of hell.
Therefore, O God, that in this life Thou plagu'st me,
Is, I confess, a portion of Thy favour.
I therefore shall bear patiently the doom
My error must work out. Then give me strength
That to the final breath of this my life
I may endure it. But my deep despair
At my calamities now moves me less,
O Father, than the fact Thy sacred name
Is scorned and mocked at by these impious dogs.
This cuts my outraged bosom to the heart.
For this, my sorry plight supplies the cause.
Is this, they say, that famous Hebrew leader
Whom his God chose as saviour of His people,
And, in whose reckless living, vain conceit
Made light of heaven's favour and so lost it?
Which is more worthy of sublimest glory,
The God of Abraham's sons or our own god,
Philistia's pride? The outcome has decided!
Dagon has triumphed as chief deity.
Thus they assail the King of heaven and earth
With foul and sinful shouts of calumny.

This bitter mockery of the impious cuts
My heart more savagely than any razor.
Now I am being led to some new sport,
While the whole city, drunk with wine, performs
Its rites in honour of a bestial idol.
Here I must stand, a theme of jest and laughter
To men and women; but the dreadful thing
Is that, with me, Thy power will be mocked.
O Majesty divine, come, castigate
These blasphemies with Thy avenging fury!

HERALD

In Dagon's honour, greatest of all gods,
Who has at last vouchsafed us victory
Over our enemies, it now is right
That all of you, assembled in this party,
Maidens and boys, Philistian men and matrons,
Should lay aside all vestiges of sorrow
And spend the festal day in glad applause.
Let harps and flutes resound and trumpets make
Exultant clamour. The Philistian leaders
Have summoned here all means of merriment.
    But why are you so sad, strongest of men?
Will your triumphant hands break off these chains?
And will the Hebrew God you fabricate
In vain imagination rescue you?
Your spirit should be filled with gratitude
At being called to share our public joys.
Will you not smooth your forehead? Take this lyre;
Its plectrum's lighter than the mill's great bar;
Rouse up your genius; chant your former battles;
Hymn, in your lay, Delilah's soft embraces!

SAMSON

Would I were haply deaf as well as blind!
Then should I not be forced to hear these mocks
And blasphemies. Alas, ye wicked lads,

Why rend my beard and hair? Ah, leave alone
My ears and nostrils. It is quite enough
To lose my eyes. Who mocks at wretched age
Has often fallen by a speedy death.
    Alas, my frame grows faint. My strength of soul
Has left me. Boy, I beg you, lead me quickly
To seek some pillar on whose massy side
My weariness may lean, lest I collapse.
    O God, high ruler of the angel hosts,
While in my wretchedness I call upon Thee
With my last words, grant favour to my prayer:
Punish through me the sinful mockeries
Heaped on Thy godhead by this impious crew!
Breathe back my former strength in these my limbs;
So may the glad, exulting celebrations,
Prepared to scorn Thy deity and honour
An evil idol, end in sad lamenting.
Here let me perish with the infidels,
But not die unavenged. 'Tis sweet to die
In such a slaughter of Thy enemies.
    Yes, all is well, but now do you, my boy,
Seek safety in the fastest flight you can.

A PHILISTINE
    Alas, we die! The pillars have been broken.
    The house is falling down!

ANOTHER   I die!

ANOTHER   I die!
    Help, help, O Dagon! Help, thrice great one!

ANOTHER   Help!

BOY
    Almighty Ruler of the angel armies,
    With what a sudden crash the roof has fallen!
    What shouts of men, what wails of women rise!

Barely this flight of mine has saved my life!
I'll go and have this arm of mine bound up,
Cracked by a falling beam. Then shall I seek
Dead Samson's mother out, to tell his deed
And all the story of her son's sad end.

(*Exit* Boy)

ACT FIVE

(*Enter* Eluma, *alone*)

Eluma

Does the revolving Sun behold a mortal
More wretched than myself, hemmed in by evils?
Alas, my son, to what a sorry plight
You have brought me, yourself, and all the sons
Of ancient Abraham! What infamy
Has stained through you the honour of Jehovah!
Had you in the great days of your success
But died amid your own heroic deeds,
How sweet to me had been your passing hence,
With your dear mother's hand to close your eyes.
What miseries of spirit I had lacked,
With all these present evils still unknown,
Even forestalled forever by your death!
But now I see the freedom of God's people
Crushed by the yoke of nameless slavery.
My son has been disgraced, imprisoned, blinded,
And, in a slavery far worse than death,
Mocked at—this flouts my ears and eats my marrow.
    But since it has seemed good to Thee to punish
My erring son, punish his body, Lord;
Burn it, Lord; break it; cut it; but, O God,
Let not his deathless soul be cast away!
    But who is this that comes with hasty step
And with his right arm wrapped in snowy linen?

(*Enter* Boy)

BOY

    Eluma, you, of all the kin of Samson,
    I wished first to address. The chance now given,
    I would declare the sequence of your woes,
    And add the grace of comfortable words.
    The hearts of women are less firm to bear,
    Than those of men, the shock of sudden grief.
    But recent terror (mark my trembling limbs!)
    Prevents my uttering meditated speech.

ELUMA

    Tell me your news, whatever it may be;
    Its weight of pain will not be unfamiliar;
    For such my earlier miseries have been
    That any added burden must be light.

BOY

    I'll tell it, light or heavy, as it happened.
    In the same prison where your son endured
    His cruel captive torments was I born
    And reared till now. The gaoler's son and heir,
    I saw men driven on with whips to toil
    Supreme and measureless, doomed to the dungeon
    For their whole life. Amid these sufferers, one
    Would loudly curse to hell his mother's womb
    That bore him for this mill of miseries.
    Another railed at heaven with his oaths
    And madly swore at daylight's lingering length
    And swore again at every morn that dawned.
    And still another, shouting terribly,
    Called on the Evil One, in hope that he
    Might sink down sudden to the pit of hell.
    Among these prisoners I used to marvel
    That Samson only, in his lot by far
    Most wretched of them all, bore horrid torment
    With a supremely calm and steadfast mind;

He even blamed his comrades' spitefulness
Since, as he said, they magnified their evils.
Let them now venture to recall that he
Had drawn these penalties upon his head,
Having provoked his God to righteous anger.
Thus he besought to show his own repentance
And to placate God's wrath with humble prayer,
Likewise to strengthen their weak minds with faith
In endless life and everlasting glory
To which a door was opened through these evils.
Nay, more, by sacred argument he turned
My own heart from vain trust in many gods
And taught me the true road to endless bliss.
This heavenly gift I never shall exchange
For all the futile bounties of the world;
God will preserve me to my dying day.
And hence me also no small grief distresses
As I recall his talks, sweeter than honey,
That I shall hear no more. Nor with dry cheeks
Can I relate to you the dreadful way
In which he perished, for it happened thus:
The leaders of the Philistines had ordered
A holiday, a solemn feast for all
In praise of Dagon, by whose holy aid
Samson had fallen. In their pagan mode,
A victim first was slaughtered on the altar;
Then came the priest's abominable prayers
And paeans chanted in triumphal fashion;
Forthwith they turn to feasts elaborate
And quaff unnumbered cups of unmixed wine,
Laying all cares aside in sport and jest.
They then decide to summon Samson forth;
They have him brought. I went along with him
Because I felt keen pity for his blindness
And joined him as a guide all-vigilant

Upon an unknown road. In zeal to gaze
A host of celebrants from all sides crowded
To pack the famous temple where he stood.
After the early courses of the feast,
An interval was called for. The whole house
Resounded with gay uproar. Flutes and timbrels,
Organs and trumpets made incessant music.
Amid all these, blind Samson stood alone,
A thing of mockery; for bands of youths
Plucked insolently at his hair and tunic
And uttered brutal jokes about his blindness.
   He bore these mockeries with agitation,
Heaving deep groans from out his inmost breast,
And breathed petitions to his Heavenly Father.
   The temple had been based upon twin columns
Of solid marble. By these stood your son;
Around one column went his right arm's grip,
His left arm grasped the other; with fresh strength,
He tore the pillars from their pediments
And with a sudden crash the building fell.
Wailing of women and the cries of men
Were lifted to the stars. Then broken stones,
Rocks, rubble and a mass of falling beams
Covered them all amid a cloud of dust.
Three thousand of both sexes had been watching
The mock of Samson (drawn there by the sport,
A gay, brief prologue to their tragedy),
To all of whom the ruin in one instant
Provided sudden death and burial too.
With no distinction there, the nation's leaders
Lay dead beside the basest of the crowd
And with them all lies your heroic son
Who wrought a greater slaughter in his death
Than all his bloody victories while he lived.
Warned of this fate, I took to hurried flight

Yet could not quite avoid all jeopardy,
Because a falling timber broke this arm.
Thus you have consolation for your son
Past counting, for he fell not unavenged
And not inglorious. Now a crowd with mattocks
Is digging out the corpses from the wreckage,
Sodden with gore, smashed brains and broken
    bodies.
The entire town resounds with lamentation.
I go to see the sequel. So, farewell.

(Exit Boy)

ELUMA

I live, as I shall die hereafter, wretched
Beyond all women. Woe is me, my son,
What sorrow you have brought your mother's heart,
In this your death, a death alas twofold!
O blessed man, who by your conversation
Are ever used to soothe my grieving breast,
Come, help me now, as quickly as you can.
The anguish of my soul can go no further.

(Enter PRIEST)

PRIEST

Death is the lot of all. Remember, death
Is closely knit to living from the hour
When life first issues from its primal source.
Man is a shade, a bubble, dust, a flower.
Does your mind marvel when a vase is broken,
 Fashioned of fragile clay or brittle glass?
I do not think it: thus all sons of earth
Are destined to expire in easy ruin.

ELUMA

You do not grasp the burden of my grief.
You speak of common things. To these long since
My heart gave numb acceptance. Greater cares

By far, alas, now weigh upon my spirit
And lie upon me like a leaden mountain.
Far better had it been, had I but lived
My life unwedded. What a fool was I,
Who once bewailed to heaven my childless bed
And gained a son by agonies of prayer!
Forsooth, I bore my baby, not to God
But to black hell, a most unhappy birth.
Alas, I am most wretched among women!

PRIEST

I gather that anxiety torments you
Over your son's salvation. He, you think,
Is lost forever, exiled from God's throne.

ELUMA

The law forbids a man to take his life,
Nor can I conjure up a crime more dire,
One that allows no respite for repentance.
Does any woman live more sad than I?

PRIEST

Eluma, lay aside your baseless fear
And cease a little from your vain complaints.
Lend me, I pray, your wonted pious ears.
I never shall deny that man commits
A crime detestable in his self-murder,
When direst desperation of the mind
Directs his hostile hands against his body
Or when his terror of impending peril
Cuts off his anxious soul before its time.
    But in your son's demise, he did not lack
Divine approval, for men testify
That ere his death he lifted prayers to heaven
And his petition suddenly was granted.
For God Himself, in that last victory,
Poured out on Samson's frame a power divine

More notable than all he knew before.
This victory shall later generations
Hand down with loftiest praise, as long on earth
As the high sun shall shed his conquering light.
Nothing with wicked hand is done by man
When God has urged it. It is laudable
To have a judge give up his blood and life
On the behalf of those set under him.
Some day, I tell you, it will come to pass
That God the Father's only Son will come,
Down from the everlasting citadel
On high in heaven, and in wondrous wise
Become the humble offspring of a virgin.
    Even as Samson with an ass's jaw
Could overthrow in strength a thousand men,
So that Messiah, with the Word divine,
Will break the power of hell, the sting of death,
The infernal head of the envenomed Serpent.
As springs of water from the jawbone's tooth
Gushed forth to quench the wearied leader's thirst
After the toil of fighting, so God's words
Refresh the broken souls whom sin oppresses
And whom the flame of heavenly anger scorches.
As Samson, by the power of his arm,
Felled a huge lion, so the Virgin's son
With heavenly strength shall crush the Prince of
    Hell.
As Samson, hemmed within the city's walls,
Tore off the gates by night and took them hence,
So Christ, shut in the cave of Tartarus,
Shall break out from that dungeon of the deep.
As Samson by his death slew many foes,
So shall the Virgin's great celestial Son
By His own death discomfit hell's battalions;
And by His blood there will return to earth

The grace we lost through our first mother's sin.
Of this stupendous work, this matchless gift,
God gives His promise in the death of Samson
As by a metaphor. Ah, when indeed,
When will that day, urged by our ardent prayers,
Dawn with its rosy light on this our world,
And God himself, the author of salvation,
Appear to mortal eyes in human form?
But see, a band of sorrowing men approaches,
Bearing dead Samson's body on a bier.

(*Enter* ATTENDANTS, *carrying the body of Samson*)

ELUMA

Hither lay down from off your grieving shoulders
Your melancholy burden, that the eyes
Of a most wretched mother may behold it.
On this last spectacle let sorrow feed.
Let showers from mine eyes provide my son
A final service. Though naught's left to do,
I would address his corpse a farewell word
And press a parting kiss on his dear mouth.
Alas, my son! In what a state, alas,
I see your filthy beard and Nazar locks
Matted with dust and blood. Upon your face
None of your former beauty has remained;
You lie a stranger to your very self
And to your mother. Pray, accept these tears,
A mother's final gift from aged eyes,
And take this kiss, and this, and this my last.
Woe to the fleeting hopes that parents wish
Their children! With how changeable a wheel
The fates of mortals rise and fall again!

PRIEST

Eluma, lay aside grief-bearing tears,
Nor, in the manner of men ignorant

Of God Almighty, men without a hope
Of life beyond the grave to buoy them up,
Vainly oppress your heart with too much mourning;
Nay, rather, recognize the will of God
By whose unchanged, inevitable law,
At the due hour that He has ordained,
A life is born, a life is blotted out.
No accident or chance brings this to pass
Without His providence. God numbers rather
Each several hair upon the human head
And none can fall without His high assent.
What the necessity of Fate commands,
That must be borne, and God not fought against.
The soul of Samson dwells mid stars of heaven,
Whence at the first it had its origin;
There, held in God's right hand, it is exempt
From every risk and every fear of danger.
As for the body foul that here lies broken
And horrid to behold in dust and blood,
When the whole universe shall end in ashes,
His flesh and bones, summoned from earth's broad
        bosom,
Shall rise, in strength renewed, to join his soul
Surpassing all the sunlight in its splendour
And capable of everlasting joy.
Think deeply on the state of our existence:
You will confess, I doubt not, that the dead
Are far more happy than they were when living.
As many evils weigh upon our heads
As are the waves upon the raging sea
Or as the stars that stud the eternal sky.
    Therefore think gravely on the proper limit
To set upon your sorrow. This your son
Has gone before. He is not lost at all;
Soon we shall follow, at our time appointed,

To join the company of those in heaven.
Ah, what great joy will then flood pious souls,
When Majesty Divine will show itself
In beatific vision; when, commingled
With choirs of the blessed, we shall taste
A deathless feast of everlasting joy;
Brothers to brothers then will be restored
Parents to children, friends brought back to friends,
And husbands to the bosoms of their wives,
Each recognizing each in highest heaven.

But Thou, O kind Creator, ever found
The glorious Champion of Thy chosen people,
Forget in peace the anger we deserve.
Repair for us the loss that we have suffered
In losing thus our chief invincible.
Fill Samson's place, raise up a mighty hero,
Armed with Thy strength, and leave us not oppressed
Beneath so foul a yoke of slavery.

But you, O little maidens, chaste descendants
Of Father Abraham, sing in Hebrew fashion
A funerary song in measures sad
While we escort him to his burial mound.
For to lament is fitting at the fall
Of this so great and notable a leader,
To match our public grief with ululation.

So it has come to pass in men's affairs
That often they must end in grievous state,
Even as lamentations, shrieks and tears
Now end the finished tragedy of Samson.

CHORUS
Sadly the death of Samson here we mourn;
Our tears from sorrowing eyes we shed forlorn;
And beat with sorrowing hands upon each breast
Filled full of bitter grief and sad unrest.

As here in solemn fate great Samson died,
The Hebrew nation's crown has lost its pride,
Its wall, its citadel, its prop, its peak,
Its post, its tower, its refuge for the weak.

Even as sheep, robbed of their shepherd's care,
Will bleat and wander trembling here and there,
An easy prey to hands of plunderers given
Or by the greedy wolf to slaughter driven,

Just so we wander, with our leader lost,
Into the hazards of dread rapine tossed
Among our enemies, so great a pack
Of troubles presses down upon our back.

The simple sheepfold of the innocent
Again must bleat its desperate lament
At slavery more grievous to endure
Than all the pangs of death's discomfiture.

All slavery is wretched, but alas
Naught in the world the evil can surpass
When wicked men of earth their rule can fling
Upon the good; a Fury is their King.

True piety in teaching is forgotten;
The nurturing of trust in tyrants rotten
Prevents it, and in time the pious breast
Drinks in barbarian manners from the rest.

If any man should purpose to retain
The sacred rites that God's pure laws ordain,
His property and person are laid bare
To perils by the thousand everywhere.

Once Thou, O mighty God, by Thy right hand
Didst lead our fathers out of Pharaoh's land,
And, in the middle of the sea, the wave
Stood up on either hand, a wall to save.

And there dread Egypt's tyrant Thou didst drown
When the swift waters of the sea came down,
The waves returning to their former state
With the grim murmur of a gurgling fate.

Our fathers then Thy leadership obey
Under the likeness of a cloud by day;
And pillared fire by night before them went
To thread the desert of their discontent.

Through forty peaceful years, while sterile earth
Refused all fruitage from its sandy dearth,
Thou gavest to our folk their daily bread,
Sent down from heaven as they marched ahead.

Moreover, at Thy bidding, flints accurst
Opened their veins and slaked our people's thirst;
While quails in companies their path bestrewed,
Filled all the camp and furnished them with food.

A blessed region, by Thy favour granted,
After our enemies had been supplanted,
Was our possession without price or money,
A land that flowed abundant milk and honey.

O Heavenly Father, once so loving-hearted,
Where has the glory of Thy grace departed?
What blocks Thy fount of goodness in its gush
That from so rich a vein was wont to rush:

Remember now Thy love for Abraham;
Let Isaac's offspring be Thy precious lamb;
And in Thy tender care remember well
Thy treaty made of old with Israel.

Who would deny that deep in human sins
Is found the motive where God's wrath begins?
With penitence of heart we here confess
The justice of Thy penalty's duress.

Smitten in heart, we raise our supplication.
With kindly face, forgive our erring nation.
Be merciful, O Father, for that word,
Is one that Thou delightest to have heard.

Hereafter by Thy spirit rule our hearts,
That through the holy laws that it imparts
Our lives obedient to Thy will may go
And Thy great glory in our actions grow!

PRIEST

Enough of lamentation. Let us now,
As needs must be, before the ocean covers
The failing radiance of the sinking sun,
Place his dead body in its burial cave.
And you, Eluma, lay aside your woe.
Those whom the fates on earth must separate
The dawn of Doomsday will unite again.

ELUMA

Although sure faith in resurrection's power
Fights against grief, yet sorrow still beleaguers
My inmost heart. No, I am confident
No day will mark a terminus to grief
Except the day that takes away my soul.

THEODORUS RHODIUS

Simson
1600, 1602, 1607, 1615, 1616, 1619, 1625
Samson

———❧———

Dramatis Personae

Acme	An old woman
Samson	A Philistine
Chorus of Jews	A soldier
Delilah	A messenger

Added in inflated edition: father-in-law, herald, chorus of Hebrew soldiers, a second messenger

PROLOGUE

The author explains, in prose and in verse, that he has added much to his earlier version in order to make it stageworthy.

In the 265 lines thus prefixed to Rhodius' first draft, Samson returns to his Timnite father-in-law and demands his bride. When told that she has been given to another, he declares war on the Philistines and destroys their crops. Handed over to the Philistines by his countrymen, he bursts his bonds and kills a thousand men with the jawbone of an ass. Later he escapes an ambush in Gaza by carrying off the gates. The Philistines promise Delilah 1,100 pieces of silver if she will ferret out the secret of his strength. An old woman helps her to dress for her night with Samson. She seeks his secret but receives a false answer.

ACT ONE

(Beginning of the *Ur-Samson*)

Samson's guardian angel, Acme by name, comes to warn him to flee from Delilah and avoid her disastrous wiles. Samson promises to obey Acme. A chorus of Jews, in formal strophe, antistrophe and epode, hail his greatness and echo her warning.

ACT TWO

Delilah pleads with the old woman for her aid in overthrowing her enemy, Samson. A Philistine reproaches her for her lack of success. She vows her devotion to the patriotic task. The chorus comments on the iniquity of women.

ACT THREE

Samson in soliloquy recapitulates his exploits against the Philistines. Although love for Delilah still moves him, he vows solemnly to leave her and to tell her nothing. Delilah, after praying to Venus, joins him and in a long temptation scene promises to divulge nothing if he confides in her. He tells her his secret and they adjourn to her bed. The chorus condemns the tyranny of love.

ACT FOUR

A Philistine and a soldier, outside of Delilah's chamber, discuss the falsity of women. The old woman enters to tell them that Delilah has won; and they at last rush in. The chorus hears from outside the outcries of Samson as he is captured and blinded.

ACT FIVE

A messenger tells the chorus the details of Samson's capture and loss of eyes. Samson is brought in and, alternating with the chorus, bewails his fate. Delilah and the Philistines mock him. The chorus closes by prophesying speedy vengeance by Samson, even though he is blind. (End of the *Ur-Samson*)

A later addition of 97 lines is translated below. I have rendered the Latin senarius into English blank verse:

PHILISTINE

> Wreathing your jocund locks with greenery,
> Give thanks to Dagon and make holiday!
> At last into our hands has come that Samson,
> That man, the sheer amazement of his age,
> Who, while he flourished, arrogant in might,
> Exulted in black slaughter. Vanquished now
> By wiles and woman's winsome words he lies,
> And pays a penalty that fits his crimes.
> A lion thus, who once had walked the fields
> In pride, at length is caught and makes submission.
> Once we lay conquered and oppressed with ills;
> But now good fortune crowns our destiny.
> So let a victim die on holy altars
> And let the joyful day be spent in feasts
> And pleasant wine, games, singing and applause.
> To give us pleasure, let that Hebrew man
> Be led beneath the temple's lofty roof.
> 'Tis sweet to see a foe taste direst evils;
> Why should the flutes and harps delay their music?
> Let us all go: make loud the courts with joy
> And let there be no lack of means of gladness.
> > (*Exit* PHILISTINE)

SAMSON

> Why does this pagan people have me summoned?
> What can a blind man give to grace the day?
> Am I a welcome butt for mocking jest,
> A laughing stock to please the enemy?
> Better to seek again the wonted spot
> Where a sad crowd bewails its sore distress
> And many prisoners are warned with lashes
> To attend their task! No further, God, I pray,
> Inflict on me the sentence of Thine anger!
> If to my grim example folk should haste,
> The enemy will say Thou art no God.

I grant my penalties befit my deeds,
And yet vain worshippers, hateful to Thee,
Should not rejoice to see Thy servant's ruin.
But what strange strength now floods into my veins?
I go—and shall gain glory by my death!
                    (*Exit* SAMSON)

CHORUS OF HEBREWS
Alas, with Samson's capture a great burden
Weighs on our shoulders: great ills hem us in.
Prostrate we lie, under foul slavery's yoke;
No hope is left for us, the wholly lost.
But why brings yonder boy so sad a face?
                    (*Enter* BOY, *as* MESSENGER)

MESSENGER
With what a crash the mighty temple fell
When its vast pillars broke! The groanings still
Are in my ears. Poor wretch, I scarce escaped
Fom death and the dark home of Proserpine.
But look, I yonder see some friends of Samson.
I shall draw near, though bringing bitter news.
Men, I have brought you word, Samson is dead.

CHORUS
Your tale is piteous. Tell us how he died!

MESSENGER
The people with their chieftains in assent
Were making holiday in praise of Dagon
And setting free their healths from lingering grief;
That their wild joy might lack no satisfaction
They had Manoah's son before them brought,
Mocked him with bitter words amid their feasting;
Women and men and children were delighted
To use the sad, blind creature for their sport:
Thus there were those who with an impious voice
Would ask the mournful man to sing soft songs:

"Ho, sing a song about your love affairs,
Your famous exploits, or your Hebrew God!"
These words he did not bear with patient heart,
But asked me straight to lead him to the pillars.
I brought him as he bade me, fearing nothing,
When I beheld a sudden startling deed.
For thus he softly prayed: "O Lord of Heaven,
Who seest all things, grant that I may finish
This final task! Though wretched I may die,
I lack not vengeance. May I rend this house,
That, though I seem to wait with empty hands,
I may avenge me on mine enemies!"
Nor was his prayer unheard, nor vain the plea
He made to God for help. For heavenly manhood
Possessed him now; I saw his strength return
And pour into his body like a tide.
The temple had stood resting on two columns
Of solid marble. With both hands he seized them
And pushed them boldly from their pediments.
I did not stay, but took to desperate flight.
The whole high roof fell down: mixed with its roar,
The screams of tumbling thousands likewise rose.
Samson himself lay dead amid the rest,
And with his death he vanquished the unconquered.
But see, a hastening crowd brings here his body.
Bury your friend with care, and weep for him.
          (*Enter those with Samson's body*)

CHORUS

Hither, bring hither, the belovèd burden,
The mangled frame; a last look would I take
And pay due honour to a man heroic.
O pitiable Samson, low you lie!
You, once the glory of a happy home,
Are carried to the grave. Accept these tears,
A tribute from your friends, oppressed by fate.

Amid our plaints, this gladdens yet our sorrow,
That you had vengeance. And the ends of earth
Will glorify alike your life and death.
And while we tend our leader's obsequies,
Israel with lamentable voice and tears
Will still profess its love for the departed.

VINCENZO GIATTINI

Il Sansone: Dialogo per Musica
1638
Samson*

———✻———

Dramatis Personae

Delilah   Prince
Captain   Samson

PART ONE

DELILAH
>   Samson is in fetters.
>   Our fears are at an end.
>   The grief of our torments
>   Has been laid low.

PRINCE
>   From his grievous exercise
>   Where, turning the heavy mill,
>   Samson grinds our harvests,
>   My orders bring him forth,

---

*Translated from the Italian by Watson Kirkconnell. An original oratorio score in intricate rhyming patterns, almost entirely in feminine rhymes, has been rendered, in default of prosodic equivalents, in free verse.

And he breathes thus for a moment,
More for my pleasure than for his repose.
Delilah, you have had a major part
In the victory over our evil foe;
Come, and for our boast and yours even more,
O glory of the Philistines, laugh at his grief.
>   For our sport and delight
>   Over him who once caused us terror,
>   And to wipe away our tears,
>   Let the eyes of a blind man
>   Bring the fair dawn of a new day.

SAMSON
>   Unhappy Samson! You are even constrained
>   By evil fortune to hide your face!
>   Ye eyes of mine that saw me victor
>   Over the shattered squadrons of the aliens,
>   Ye arms of mine that made our foes
>   Submissive to my race,
>   And ye wild beasts that once I mastered,
>   A marvel ye have made me, past myself.
>   How do ye suffer, O mine eyes?
>   How, O my arms, do ye surrender:
>   If not that in your yielding I am punished more;
>   And in not seeing me, ye suffer more;
>   In, as it were, my greater martyrdom,
>   Samson has now no strength but to endure.
>   O Heaven offended by my deeds,
>   I yet shall gladly suffer as you wish,
>   So that, if you in truth are not unarmed,
>   Yet in dispensing me this time for grieving
>   You still show courtesy.

CAPTAIN
>   Breezes that wafted once to Hebrew plains
>   On the winds' wings

The news of our defeat in Samson's name,
Blow yet again of other happenings
Of outrage not believed in Israel.
Samson in chains laments; our laurels now
Shadow his cypresses, and where he lies
The rainbow arch of peace salutes our arms.
　　By cutting off his hair she bound
　　The hand that smote so many;
　　She who through them found out the key to
　　　　fate
　　Has changed our fortunes thus.

PRINCE

　　If chance were but to grant his former strength,
　　What slaughter of the Philistines
　　Would Samson not inflict! Now he would make
　　　　pretence
　　In empty sport and jest that he
　　Offered no danger to the Philistines.
　　Samson, stir up to fight your heart of fire,
　　If you in aught of honour are concerned,
　　Turn here your arm—a lion would attack you.
　　Come, interrupt his roaring,
　　Run on his jaws and in your stern assault
　　Feed our glad vision and your own grim thoughts.
　　Imagine for yourself his futile struggle,
　　Rend his dead body—in the arena here
　　Give us a spectacle of vanquished pride.

SAMSON

　　Unmastered monster, dauntless and untrembling,
　　Thus I shall slay you, thus intrepidly.

DELILAH

　　No, Samson, no! Feign that the fighting lion
　　Is now already dead; and if a generous instinct
　　Can draw forth sweetness from his strength,

From his imprudent jaws suck forth
Comb honey and so satisfy thyself.
Even pretended sweetness can be pleasant.
    Samson thus sucks
        From the strong one's lips
        Such blessed sweetness
        As heaven sends you down.
        If then your heart rejoices
        At such sweetness,
        With steadfast ardour
        I shall ever love you.

SAMSON
    Delilah, you deceiver,
    You were in truth the traitorous cause
    Of my bitter misfortune;
    But the dearer you were to me,
    The more is the offence and bitter savagery
    Of your derision.
    In the honey of a feigned love
    Within my bosom, the fierceness
    Of your poison proves all the greater.
        The more I pretend to such honey
            The more I shall shed my tears in rivers,
            As if, to make more harsh
            My cruel lot,
            Every bee were to change
            Its honey to a sting.
    Ah, in pity change
    Your laws to me, O Tyrants;
    Torment not thus my griefs
    With so calamitous an idea.

CAPTAIN
    So, so right are you,
    Invincible champion;

Alter then the scene,
Bring to this arena instead
The burned and wasted Philistine crops—
That was your work; scattered through them
You sent foxes round
With a thousand flames for our loss.
    Now rejoice, O Victor,
        At the past prowess of your proud heart
        For our disaster, you were thus
        The cruel cause of all this grief.

PRINCE
    Scorn now the record of such evil work,
    The memory of our losses,
    Inciting you to glory, not to grief.
    Rise up, O Samson, let it be your vaunt
    To flee unhampered from our guarded walls,
    To ward off your misfortune, you lifted up
    The gates of Gaza, and in fleeing us,
    The Night, who was your comrade, loved your zeal.
        The darkness of your eyes
        Are a rebuke to the counsel
        That was an escort to such zeal;
        And in place of that gloom
        That your faults once shadowed forth
        Night proves your mistake.

SAMSON
    Your words, O Philistines,
    Are biting but most just,
    Yet none the less unworthy
    Your glories are; first you should blush
    To see your shameful deeds
    And then confront with these
    The ideal of your fates;
        You vanquished me by guile, and not by strength.

Hope flatters me that some day
Heaven will have pity
On Samson, at whom you laugh.
The grief that you perceive in me
Is the source from which I hope it;
As for that zeal that swells in you,
My thought certainly declares
That some day it will be punished.

PART TWO

PRINCE

Crown your locks with olive leaves,
Set your hand to the plectrum, your foot to the
    dance,
Philistines arise, and with festive pantings
Of joy, reverence and faith,
Proceed with me to our liberating god.
Let the altars of Dagon be your goal.
    From eyes that once shed tears
        Let the heart's happiness flash forth
        And in the footprints that sorrow left
        May joy and laughter ever walk.

CAPTAIN

But what shall we do with Samson?

PRINCE

Let him be left at the foot
Of that venerable pillar,
And let him hear our songs
Even if he cannot see;
Let him hear, and in our more abundant joy
Let his grief be all the more abased with scorn.

DELILAH

Sound on your lyres and drums,
Rise up to the dance,

Set your feet to the ballet.
I first in these wheelings
In which my torments are set free,
Offer a pledge of my faith.

SAMSON

Alas, how much to the inward eye,
If not to my glance, the scene is revealed
In the Philistines' deeds.
You are blind, O Samson, and yet you discern
From the voice and the foot
The arrogance of the heart that surpasses in these.
Abandoned triumphs, usurped crowns,
You wound too much
My afflicted bosom.

By the glories of the past
That I bewail in their eclipse,
Present sufferings
Are doubled torment
And doubled poison.

Delilah now proposes
To eternalize the scorn of my chains;
Hence with a worse lot bring it to pass
That death may swallow up my life;
Sate yourself yet, O Tyrant, and in your dance
Make my death central to my sighs.

CAPTAIN

Prince, the view is more pleasant
For our contentment,
The more Samson faints in his pain;
But his eloquent lament
Makes one suspect in him a plotting heart,
And the more his grief expresses resentment,
Although he is vanquished in the snare,
The more his thoughts cause terror,

Lest his strength be not wholly extinguished
But is only sleeping.

PRINCE

Let him do what he can; the Philistines will do
Whatever pleases them. Do you, Delilah, harvest
The fruits of your victory, and in the arena
Express our joy and make grief prisoner.

DELILAH

His loss of hair, his dread and his lament
Are prizes, profits won and trophies due
To this my eye, my lip, and to my curls.
Thus to a look, to a voice, to a risk,
In the strongest of the Hebrew nation
The boast, the strength and the destiny surrenders.
But elsewhere blood from the slain victims
Of the woolly flock floods the ground,
And from the lifeless herd
The flame everywhere abounds in the holocaust.
To thee, great Deity, who hast preserved us
In our disputes with Israel,
The spoils of the most fearful warrior
As victim I hang up in the temple.
Behold the symbol of his conquered strength,
The sign of thy power, behold the hair!
Such glory is ascribed to Thee.
May Samson thus be confounded.

CAPTAIN AND PRINCE

Long live Delilah!

SAMSON

Do my indignities yet grow? Assuredly
My injuries are an offence to my Lord.
I know that from my follies
And my impure desires
The first fault was born; and now shall they last

Without restraint
To exceed all measure?
And so a gift from God's own hand,
Even to myself,
The hair I kept not: to a mad deity
It will be given in her rash desire.
Alas, Lord, defend Thy cause in me,
Arouse desire, kindle my strength within me.
   Already, O my God, I feel
      My vanished valour
      Flood into my heart.
      O Thou whom they have scorned in me,
      Cause me to batter down these marble pillars,
      So may I have the mighty arms
      Of both Thine anger and Thine honour.

PRINCE
   Alas, the walls are shaking.

DELILAH
   The floor is shifting.

CAPTAIN
   The altar is trembling.

PRINCE
   Ye Gods, what a strange event!

DELILAH
   What new disaster
   Is coming upon the Philistines?

CAPTAIN
   Whatever will it be, if you are causing it,
      O Samson?

SAMSON
   Lord, if Thou art the author
   Of this great thing that stirs and churns my heart,
   My spirit that resolves to come to Thee,

Graciously take away my painful dread
And cause one tomb alone
To enclose my body and my enemies.
In this conviction I console myself,
That my soul's destiny is not as theirs.
I turn to grasp you now, foul marble pillars!
Come hither, Philistines, to arms, to arms!

PRINCE

Alas! Ye Heavens! Lo, the tremblings
That the shaking earth repeats
The templed frame can no more tolerate;
From repeated shakings
The gleaming walls are shattered,
The foundations open up.
Mercy, immortal Gods!
I reflect on such great evils
In the terrible insult; I grow aware
Of the crowds and the uproar;
Vain and cut off is all escape,
Hope is already gone
As ruins crash together
Over the stumbling victims, till they form
A prison for the living, for the dead a tomb.

SAMSON

Fear not, O Philistines, the guilty martyr.
I shall not live your foe, but die with you.

CAPTAIN

To me, to whom, half dead,
The common downfall
Leaves but a few brief moments,
What more remains? If not in these events
To recognize the Philistines' lost joys
And punishment upon the arrogance
Of a lascivious heart—and generous sufferings

Of a strong man who matched himself with Death.
With my own tears and with the blood of others
I'll write upon the earth: Samson lies here.
He at a single stroke gained vast revenge
And died amid the wreckage.
In truth his glories here are infinite
Where after all his strife he lies at peace.

JOOST
VAN DEN VONDEL

Samson, of Heilige Wraeck, Treurspel
1660
Samson, or Holy Revenge*

—⁓⁓—

The tragedy is based on the Book of Judges and the fifth book
of Josephus' *History of the Jews*. The scene is at Gaza, at the
temple of Dagon, beside the court. The play begins before dawn
and ends with sunset.

Dramatis Personae

Dagon, *the prince of the abyss,*
the greatest of all the idols
(false gods) of the Philistines
The attendant of Samson
Samson, *the governor and*
judge of Israel
The chorus of Jewish women
The Prince of Gaza

The Princess of Gaza
The High Priest of the
Philistines
The soothsayer of Akkaron
The (temple) musicians
The messenger
Samson's kindred
Fadaël, *Samson's birth-angel*

ACT ONE
(*Enter* Dagon)

DAGON

I, who in Sheol wield an iron sceptre,
Corroded half with rust, and at hell's court

*Translation by Watson Kirkconnell from the Dutch of Vondel. Rhymed
Alexandrine couplets in the original dialogue have been rendered by blank
verse. Rhymed strophes are retained in the choruses.

Propose and bring to pass what may befit
The service of the kingdom of the dark,
Come here to Gaza, favourite retreat
Of spirits who on bat-wings wheel in air,
To help to celebrate this festival,
Joining the great procession with my lackeys,
Who stink of brimstone, foul with soot and dirt,
And comb with hooded claws my shaggy locks,
All venomous adders, fierce and full of spite
As if aroused from out the red-hot nest,
The deep, sulphuric pool, to honour me.
From underneath the throne my voice may come,
Or in this holy temple I may speak,
Where Dagon's priesthood to the altar walks
With reverence and pours out bullock's blood
In honour of my dark divinity,
Offering oblations to the Prince of Night,
With welcome jubilation, songs of triumph,
And sacrificial shows in which we spirits
Take much delight. What pleasure it will be
When in the presence of our majesty
The arch-foe Samson will be led in triumph,
Blinded and fettered with a double chain,
Dragged up the street and smitten busily,
Lashed by the guard who steers him, who with links
Of bridle fetters drives or reins him in,
So that he rises or sinks fainting down
And sweat-drops dribble down his haggard face.
In this my servants revel, while the Jew,
The plague and curse of my community,
Gives vent to sighs and groans. What have they
        suffered,
These twenty years and longer, from this judge,
Who led the Jewish cities everywhere
And freed them from our yoke, that had endured

Full forty years with pain and suffering!
So well his strength availed him, fatal gift
Now shorn away completely with his hair.
The lion tamer, by a woman tamed,
Lies meekly, like a lamb, within his cage,
Dusty with flour till he scarce can breathe.
Like some fierce dog, gnashing his teeth with spite,
He eats his meals with snarling. How betimes
He plagued us, boldly slaying thirty men
At Askalon, then stripped off all their garments,
Departing with his plunder! Even worse
Was it when, to the havoc of five realms,
He tied three hundred foxes, tail to tail,
With fireworks of resin, flax and sulphur.
By this he spread the fire among the corn,
Whither they went to flee their flaming torment.
The hungry conflagration, driven on
By a strong wind, turned all the harvest land
For many leagues into a sea of fire;
And drove to tears my myriad worshippers,
Five capitals, and all the coastal plain.
The vineyard missed its seasonable grape,
The olive tree its fruit, the corn its ear.
From Gaza unto Gath the seacoast groaned,
Where our knights-templar were in woeful want
Of incomes, temple taxes, and oblations.
Then when a man of Timnath robbed this plague
Of his due wife, the whole land suffered outrage.
And though the Philistines, to right the wrong,
Consumed both sire and daughter in one fire,
He did not cease to slay them out of vengeance,
And broke them, neck and bone. The Philistines,
Wrathful with reason, came to make fierce war
Upon the Jews, who all excused themselves,
And of their own accord, to justice moved,

Bound him and brought him to his enemies.
Then, by his strength, he brake his cords like flax
And with an ass's jawbone turned and slew
A thousand heroes. Here at last he came
To couch in Gaza in a harlot's bed.
Men shut the gates. The villain, wild and false,
Rose up by night and took the city gate
Like some light feather on his mighty back,
Walking to Hebron, where he laid it down
Upon a hill beneath a rock. In vain
Men bound him many a time with tow and cord
Until his mistress sheared his seven curls
The brood-nest of his strength. We, through her guile,
Were masters, not neglectful to pierce out
His eyes, and scourge him. We in Gaza now
Sit fast and set at naught Jerusalem.
The power of Dagon grows and waxes mighty.
We go to plague the Jews, to levy tribute,
Due recompense to pay for our lost harvest.
The court of Dagon still with reason fears
The spirit of our ancient enemies,
The Jews, who with procession and God's ark,
Call for revenge and threaten once again
To break the neck of our divinity,
Dashing it from the altar, wherefore I,
In mute hostility, shall fight against them.
All Philistines today, with varnished veils
And holy guise, shall mock the Jewish folk
In Samson, who so long suppressed our power.
The circumcizèd breed, who fell long since
To our inheritance as slaves, but oft
Have bred oppressors, ravaged goods and men,
And in the name of piety and right
Murder and harry, desecrate and burn
And break our images, shall see today

That Dagon's power can rule that mighty one
Who with a jawbone dared to bruise to death
Our terrible and lofty race of giants.
Let each assume his post: we go to take
Our place in th' old, hell-consecrated idol.
(*Exit* DAGON. *Enter* SAMSON *and* ATTENDANT)

ATTENDANT

Go forth, blind Jew! Now is no time for weeping.
It is a favour granted thee today
That thou may'st pause to breathe. It seems the princes
And all the towns shall gather here together
For the land's feast of triumph. Thou, forsooth,
Shalt grace the gathering in thy blindness here
And walk in chains before our sanctuary,
Dusty with flour. Bear it all with patience,
Although the people mock. It is enough
That thou dost grind not on this holiday.
If someone comes to laugh at thee, and thou
Dost wish to dance, thou shalt be given leave
To beg for coins, or meat, or wheaten crusts.
If thou wouldst ascertain what sounds thou hearest,
Ring thou the bell about thy neck. Perchance,
Thou may'st procure a gift from pure compassion,
To meet thy plight, full of distress and sorrow.
This is thy favour for the holiday.

SAMSON

I breathe the air. Ah, tell me, is it night?
Shines now the crescent moon?

ATTENDANT   Why no, the sun
From the horizon on the countryside
Shines on men worthier to behold the day
Than Samson, who has lost life's consolation.

SAMSON

Where do I grope my way? To south, or east?

ATTENDANT

> To Dagon's temple here, beside the palace,
> Where oaks o'ershade the ground and stretch great
>   arms
> Into the air above. Now follow me,
> And by thy neckchain-ring I'll tether thee
> Upon this hollow oak, in whose recess
> Thou canst, if mocked at, hide, and sulk in peace.
> Thou mayest if thou wilt, go in and out
> And ring thy beggar's bell to ask for alms;
> I, meanwhile, at the court, must carry out
> The orders of thy warden, as is fitting.
> Thou must show good behaviour, or this lash
> Will greet thy carcass with abundant strokes,
> For pain holds evil natures in restraint.
> Do not misuse our mercy. If thou fleest,
> And dost not get away (a vain attempt!)
> We'll make thy blind eyes weep most cruelly.
> We would, by whipping thee with bundled rods,
> Make thy hard task still harder, while we fed thee
> With mouldy oaten crusts or sawdust porridge.
> And after meals thou shouldst bear firewood
> And split it, as a remedy for spleen.
> I go now, to the court, where I am summoned.
>   (*To sentries off stage*)
> Ye sentries, hold you here beside the temple.
> The Prince will hold you surety for this man.
> Iron is sometimes marred by gold and guile.
> A captive may surmise that caution sleeps.

(*Exit* ATTENDANT. *Enter* CHORUS *of young Jewish women*)

CHORUS

> *Strophe*
> Shyly we come, without bravado,
> And timid stand upon one side;
> Within the temple oak-trees' shadow

'Twere good that Hebrew girls should hide.
Too well the men of Gaza know us.
How splendid is this mighty fane!
The city swarms with folk below us,
The subjects of Philistia's reign.
How like a queen this palace marches!
What shining galleries we see!
With marble pillars, rearing arches
To the proud vault's sublimity!
This temple, what great race could plan it,
Touching the stars! What strength immense
Has hewn these ashlars out of granite
To build with full magnificence!
Ah, if God's love this way might straighten!
Ah, if they would not serve dark Satan,
Nor Ashtaroth, nor Dagon's clod,
But the sole Being, Jacob's God!

Antistrophe

God favours us, unworthy mortals,
And not these lords of quarried stone.
For what avail strong walls and portals,
Armour and weapons? God alone,
By us acknowledged, has protected
The folk He chose. No edifice
Of gold and marble, high erected,
Can pleasure those who turn from this,
Eschewing temple songs, the clinking
Of harps and shawms to idols' praise;
Their incense they consider stinking;
Oblations, pomp, and glittering ways
Of idol cults and pagan nations
Displease them. But today, alas,
Men shall behold abominations!
And how shall we, in grief's morass,
Behold the priests and princes flouting

The captive Samson with their shouting.
Ah, what a fate God's hero stains,
Fallen and caught in Dagon's chains!

ACT TWO
(*As before,* CHORUS *and* SAMSON)

CHORUS

What bell may't be that we hear clinking yonder?
Who beckons us from out that hollow tree?
Who seems to call? Come, let us all go thither,
Who, in this oak, sits lonely and alone?
He seems to ask for alms, quite overcome
With bitter poverty.

SAMSON   Have pity now!
God bless, God guard you all, whoe'er ye be!
Console and help me here in this sad state,
A poor blind man, fast shackled by the neck,
Fettered and covered with an old rough cloak,
Dull and worn out with toil, and mortified
With dust and sweat and stench unspeakable.
This is the court of Samson, lately prince
And governor and judge of a thousand thousands,
And now, alas, too lamentably fallen.

CHORUS

God guard us all! Ah, fate beyond all cure!
How can we be resigned, how swallow this?

SAMSON

Oh stay! Ye need not be ashamed, nor shun me,
Your countryman perhaps, for by your speech
It seems that ye are of the Hebrew race,
And of the tribe of Dan. Come somewhat nearer.
As by its murmur I can tell, a brook,
A living spring flows here. If anyone

Has cup or bowl, I beg her for a drink
That I may cleanse my throat and breathe again.
So many months, imprisoned here in chains,
I have toiled wretchedly within the mill,
Blind (as ye see), beaten, and snarled upon.

CHORUS
Drink from this bowl.

SAMSON   How was my heart distressed,
Stifled with dreadful thirst! Of all my ills
And torments, thirst is bitterest of all.
Once, through God's power, from an ass's tooth
A spring gushed forth, and I, from slaying hot,
Slaked my dry heart and drank. And even thus,
This wondrous spring hath succoured my distress.
May heaven bless you for your kindly hearts!

CHORUS
Prince Samson, virtuous prince, what pain we feel
To find thee in this lamentable state!
For we are Jewish women, gathered here
From east and west, and to this feast we come
To seek and comfort thee, as time permits
But not as freely as our hearts would wish.
Naught is more shameful than a thankless mortal;
That we know well, in debt to thee for help,
Service and honour. O our folk's defender,
Bear now thy grievous sufferings patiently
To what end God provides! Although the sun
Refuses thee his light, God can illume
Thy heart with inner radiance that outshines
The rays of myriad suns. For who can limit
The Almighty's power? He who so wondrously
Endowed thee with strength hidden in thy hair,
Is mighty, if He will, to arm thee now,
Even without thy hair to strengthen thee

To break the tiger's claws that work thee woe.
Tell us, however, how this fate o'ertook thee,
Deserted by thy strength. We heard the tale
In ill confusion. All the land is stirred
To hear of this thy fall that hath re-echoed
From Dan to far Beersheba. Every Jew
Hath sat in grief for thee, despoiled and outraged.

SAMSON

Would I had shunned Philistia's womankind,
Deceitful beasts! Well may I rue the day
When I, near Sorek, loved the fair Delilah,
Fickle and sly and loveless. For to drift
At the mercy of a mistress is to sail
In reckless danger on a silent sea.
Seduced by my foes' money, night and day
She clung to me, demanding that I tell her
The secret of my strength, and even pled
Amid the hottest fires of our love,
A soul storm seldom weathered by a man.
Alas, had then my spirit been as strong
As this my frame, I should have held my peace
And told her nothing. Yet I knew enough
To dupe her scheming thrice with bold pretence:
That with green withes she tie me, or with ropes—
Seven ropes, never used—or weave my hair
In seven locks and bind them into one,
Nailed straitly to the wall. God's enemy,
Springing from ambush, shot too short three times.
Then she thus grappled me and boarded me,
As opening her heart: "O perjured nature,
How can I love thee, who dissemblest thus
Thy heart from me, and to my questionings
Dost never give true answer: Though thou beest
Devoted to Jehovah, ev'n from birth;
Though razor ne'er hath sheared thy shaggy head;

Though thou restrain thyself from wine's delight;
Though thou art circumcized and followest
Thy father's laws that circumcize the child;
And though thou wilt not try forbidden food—
All this I shall concede thee. I'll not ask
That thou from Moses' customs shouldst depart.
Preserve thy usage, offer up thy prayers
To thy strange deity, who, in a tent,
Is guarded by his priests within an ark.
But show me where thy law would have thee lie
And cheat a lovely woman whose affection
Honours thee greatly, lulling thee to sleep.
Is this fidelity to me, thy mate,
The fairest woman of all Palestine,
Who hath refused herself to lords and princes?
What wealth thou hast, what friendship thou enjoyest
Through intercourse with me, plucking with joy
The flower of my prime, my rose of youth,
In life's fair dawn! I offered thee my limbs,
This figure marble-white from head to toe,
This body, fitter for the royal bed
Of the great kings of Askalon or Gath
Or Akkaron or Gaza or Azotus.
Thou hast enjoyed me, though my country cried:
'She hath embraced a Jew, our sorest Plague!
Her youth has been frustrated by a Jew!'
How fine is now my state! O wicked trifler,
O trickster, shall one treat one's dearest thus?
Shall I, who gave thee all, be given naught?
Thou art the country's judge; thou judgest wrong;
Go now to the tribunal with thyself.
Is this thing just? And wouldst thou thus offend
Against thy dearest, yea, thy truest one?
How would thy hard heart then maltreat a stranger,
Some woman whose pale beauty, beside mine,

Is a mere shadow and a mockery?
Where hast thou ever found my like in Dan,
Or Ephraim? I tell thee I am worthy
That choicest men should angle for my love
And hold me in respect. If thou may'st say
An angel once foretold thee to thy parents
A true, God-consecrated son, who came
To them as promised, let thy utterance crown
Thy holiness and not defame its merit!
If thou by some high spirit were conducted
To be thy people's leader, cease these tricks!
Yea, let Judge Samson's word be like a seal!"

CHORUS
    The flatterer would move a heart of stone!

SAMSON
    Still I stood bravely out against the storm,
By night and day, and neither gave nor yielded.
Then into tears of crocodiles she burst,
And made an uproar. Early in the morn,
Inflamed with hot desire she caught me then,
And vowed her love, with tears upon her cheeks
That gave her rosy face a nobler glow,
Like a spring rose, fed by a crystal stream,
But with a might not found in any flower.
Tears are a lovely woman's readiest weapon
When she despairs of getting what she wants.
A sudden death she threatened for herself
Frighting my heart. Then, weeping, she burst forth:
"Go, cruel one! Embrace a dearer mate!—
Thou whom my pleasures have so little swayed
That thou deniest an ear to my complaints
And wilt not open up thy heart to me.
Sworn foe of all our altars, of our gods
And temples, touch me not! Henceforth, no Hebrew

Shall touch, unhurt, this dimpled alabaster,
This snow beveined with blue, my cheek's fair flower,
This blossom freshly opened in the dew
Of Palestine; for I'll not suffer it.
Take thy face elsewhere, for thou art unworthy
That my eyes' diamond light should shine on thee.
Thou hast in vain drunk greedily my love,
And like a hypocrite didst ravish me
Again and yet again, and tousled me,
Kissing my cheeks, my bosom, and my lips,
And I kissed thee as hotly in return,
And fondled and caressed thee in my arms
Until I slaked the frenzy of thy flames.
That hast thou lost unworthily. Depart,
Out of my sight, thou who seducest maidens!"

CHORUS

Oh, hadst thou timely torn thyself away!

SAMSON

My heart was blind with love; and all her sobbing
Grieved me to death. Continual lamentation
Softened my heart like wax. The water-drop
Thus conquers the hard granite. At the last
I let myself be moved, and made confession,
How that my strength, through miracle of God,
Lay in my unshorn hair. She swore by Dagon
That this her mouth to no one would betray.
Nevertheless, there rained into her lap
A shower of silver coin, wherewith my foes
As with a dagger, pierced my mistress' bosom
And readily seduced her fickle heart.
With doom at hand, I trusted in her word.
She granted me the limit of delight
And let me snore, sated in her embrace,
Dead drunk in soul and body with her love.

Meanwhile in silence (may God punish her!)
The razor shore away my seven locks.
I awoke, but ah, too late. The enemy
Burst eager through the doorway and made haste
To bore my eyes out and to chain me fast
And dragged me here to Gaza, where I shrink,
Doomed to my prison toil and mocked by all.

CHORUS

O prince of Israel, champion of the righteous,
How altered is the state to which thou'rt come!
What dost thou ask of us? We stand here ready
To serve thee still. Reveal thy grieving heart!

SAMSON

My guard is coming back without delay.
But my hair grows again. I lie in wait
To avenge myself upon the heathen race,
Yea, earlier than men dream. By night the Spirit
Hath shown a means to free myself from bonds.
Be of good cheer, and wail not. My discharge
Is now at hand. Triumphant death, at which
The world shall stir, hangs over Samson's head.
Not long shall he grind corn, mocked at and plagued
By every sex and age, for with their lives
They shall pay deadly for this toil of mine.
This do I bid you, that when I shall die
Men shall concede to me a funeral
And burial within my fathers' tomb.
Promise me, each of you, to keep this pledge.

CHORUS

Alas, poor prince, heaven will strength thee.
And we would hope that it may never be
That thou shouldst slay thyself with thine own hand.

SAMSON

I shall not stain my hands upon this body
But nobly, like God's hero, end my life

So that the earth and sea shall both be moved.
Be not afraid when ye shall hear the means
By which the enemy was brought to doom.

CHORUS

Since thou diest nobly, mirror of the brave,
We shall inter thy bones beside Manoah
And cheer thy fathers' ashes with thy body,
If it is in our power. Take as token
And seal of faith the hand of all these women.
May heaven punish her who fails her word!
Receive, our country's prince, these silver pieces
To serve thee in thy need, alas, alas!

SAMSON

Keep now your gift. I look for happier hours.
If I am poor, it will not last for long.

CHORUS

Command us freely: we are here to serve thee.

SAMSON

Take care, where'er ye wander, that no Jew
Be found at all today in Dagon's temple.
Ye shall perhaps, along the streets and markets,
Meet with the news of this unholy feast,
Ordained in triumph that the proud may laugh
At captive Samson with their choruses
And lead him round about in their procession.

CHORUS

Thy subjects long to see their prince again,
Even in this sad state.

SAMSON   'Tis very well.
But let them look through trellices, from roofs,
Or out of windows. It doth not befit
The race that burns a holy offering
To great Jehovah's praise to mingle here
Amid idolatry, where Gaza dances

To bells and drums before the black high altar
Of Dagon, and among the banqueters,
Devotes lascivious sport to honour him.
Such calumny avoid. And in our name
Command, as we are zealous for the law,
That no Jew set his foot in Dagon's temple,
Lest God reveal Himself, as in the past,
And by a miracle should smite the roof
Of the accursed building with His thunders.
I do not now tell all my guardian angel
Foretold to me by night about this feast.
(*Enter* ATTENDANT)

ATTENDANT
Jewesses, have ye found the prince so soon?

CHORUS
We find a prince whose neck is bound with chains,
Who, with his eyesight gone, is doomed to toil
Within a prison mill. O what a shame
To trample on a conquered hero thus,
To make him toil! 'Tis unjust and past reason.

ATTENDANT
We slaughter him, who with a jawbone slew,
Who drove the tail-tied foxes through our corn
And turned to wilderness and waste and desert
As fair a realm as e'er the sun may shine on.
Your fathers put their brother in a pit,
Then sold him as a slave, bereaving thus
Their agèd father, who long mourned for him,
Supposing that a wild beast had destroyed him.

CHORUS
Thence came the rise of Joseph, who in time
Was chosen governor beside the Nile.

ATTENDANT
'Tis true, he came to honour, set so high.
He did not owe his brothers any thanks.

CHORUS

> Into what sorrow has his mistress brought him,
> Sold and betrayed while in the depths of sleep!
> He was not overcome in open fight.

ATTENDANT

> So rightly fare those impotent to turn
> From beautiful and faithless paramours.
> Now it is time to go, before the crowd
> Gathers along the streets. Ye cannot help
> His grief by weeping. Now the court has ordered
> That he be kept confined for further counsel.
> As I was bid, I tied the blind man fast
> To this tree with his chains. Now am I sent
> Back to the gaol again with him. My watch
> Is set above him. He is all my care.
> What ill constraint is service at the court!
> Something is always wanting. Now the rope
> Is far too long, and then again too short.
> So is it now with me: I brought him out.
> And presently they drive us in again.

CHORUS

> Pardon, we beg thee, for the poor blind man!

ATTENDANT

> Why do ye ask of me? Here comes the Prince,
> Who can, if it so please him, lift this yoke
> Or make it heavier. I do my duty:
> I was commanded to depart. But go,
> Speak to the Prince! Perhaps he'll grant your favour.

CHORUS (*To* SAMSON)

> Thy heart God strengthen, ere it die of grief!

(*Exit* SAMSON *and* ATTENDANT. *Enter* PRINCE OF GAZA)

PRINCE

> The mighty concourse from the countryside
> Into the city saw the sun this morning
> Rise in the east, hung with funereal clouds;

At which men feared lest thunderstorm or shower
Should mar the feast of Dagon at its height,
And quench the altar fires, in triumph kindled
To burn a hecatomb of snow-white bullocks,
And please the deity with grateful pomp,
While Palestine's oppressor feels our power
In chains. The weather yet can change, in faith;
The sky turn clear. But who are these who come
Our festival to honour? Hebrew girls
They all would seem, joyless and dull and timid.
Their heads hang on one side. Their hearts are sunk
In deep dejection. 'Tis no wonder, surely.
We have at last subdued the mighty foe
Under our claws. The news resounds abroad.
And hark, the sound of chains, where he departs,
Stinking in his captivity! They come here.

CHORUS

Your Grace, forgive us for approaching you
To make request. Pray, pardon this presumption.

PRINCE

Ye Hebrew maidens, wherefore do ye weep?
Hath anyone abused you? Here the court
Protects each one, defending by its justice,
Shows favour to the good, requites the evil.
This court has no regard for race or person.

CHORUS

'Tis right, Your Grace. So shall a kingdom stand.
Yet, none the less, a prince were far from wrong
If he mixed mercy with severity
Towards one who merits strictest punishment.
We, at report of this triumphal feast,
Have come to Gaza, with the hope that we
Might influence the powers of Palestine,
With our laments, to merciful regard

For our strong judge, fall'n in a pit of hate,
From high to low, and not without some reason.
Your towns have suffered loss irreparable,
Loss that has wounded five chief cities' lives.
But the unpitying fate that now is his,
The loss of vision, in a night of darkness,
This surely is to lose the half of life!
Bereft of strength, he suffered a half-death
When foemen bored out both his anguished eyes
And led him here in chains through jubilant streets.
Even the hearts of those whom he had wronged
Were stirred to some compassion. Mingle then,
Although 'tis late to ask you, yet a drop
Of mercy with your justice. Let revenge
Be now abated. There will follow you
The honour of forgiveness to a foe.

PRINCE

When your chief tribe, whose standard bears
        the lion,
Crossed over our cold Jordan, and in rout
Drove King Adonibezek from the field,
They seized him in his flight and hacked the thumbs
From off his hands and feet. Then was he forced
Like some vile dog to gather up from earth
With his own mouth the crumbs that daily fell
Out of the dish, to crawl on hands and feet,
To wallow and to rummage in the dust,
Until, led to Jerusalem with joy,
He died in fetters, yielding up his life.

CHORUS

Because he had himself maltreated thus
Seventy rightful kings, they ruthlessly
Allowed his tyranny to last no longer.
His doom was fitting, after nature's law.

PRINCE

Then Samson cannot reasonably complain.
He who plagues others, should himself be plagued.

CHORUS

If money can redeem him, name your price.

PRINCE

Here justice is not bought. 'Tis not our practice
Nor does one give a foe a chance for vengeance.

CHORUS

Our prince is blind and sits deprived of sight.
Thus powerless, he dreams of no revenge.

PRINCE

He is our warning beacon to the wicked.

CHORUS

His loss of sight is warning in itself.

PRINCE

He has been sentenced to perpetual chains.

CHORUS

You are not pledged to perpetuity.
The same authority condemns and frees.

PRINCE

Offend a sentence not yet long endured?

CHORUS

The sentence stands. But let him break away.

PRINCE

How can that happen, with regard for justice?

CHORUS

Men, when they would connive, peep through
    their fingers.

PRINCE

Men are too wanton and would mark the deed.

Why strengthen bad men in their wickedness,
To go their old way, neighbours to affliction?

CHORUS
Freedom for Samson would not please the wicked.

PRINCE
First shall ye feel the impact of our power.
We shall not rest with Samson's punishment.
It is decided to invade Judaea
And levy tribute from all Jewish tribes
As far as flowing Jordan, or perchance,
To ravish all the land with blood and fire.
Moreover, we shall claim arrears of tribute
These twenty years so spitefully withheld
By Samson's proud command and lawless strength.

CHORUS
Would you thus plague God's folk's inheritance?

PRINCE
Inheritance?

CHORUS   Since Canaan was possessed
By Abraham eight hundred years ago.
This was the people that Jehovah blest
And brought in wealthy numbers out of Egypt.

PRINCE
Ye'll shamelessly astonish everyone,
Glorying thus, for Egypt ye had pillaged,
Robbed of its treasure. And a rood of land
Was all Chaldean Abraham possessed
At Mamre when he came, a foreigner.

CHORUS
The patriarch Abraham fought valiant wars,
Defeated kings, and saved his kinsman Lot.
Then Abraham's descendant rescued Egypt,
Fed by his bounty. They did thank a stranger

That pangs of hunger did not slay them all.
To us our fathers' God gave fruitful Canaan.

PRINCE

He gave it you? To whom! A wicked gang
Of murderers, born enemies of gods,
Temples, and altars—crude iconoclasts
Who spare not temple choirs nor sanctities!
Hungry and fierce, ye came in from outside
And thrust legitimate princes from their thrones
And ancient realms. Then, by this spirit driven,
Ye made new laws, whose rigours rack'd the
          conscience.
And now, your judge, for whom ye speak and plead,
Has laid the land in ashes worse than ever.

CHORUS

Forgive it, mighty Prince. We can't deny it.
We merely came to pray to you for mercy.

PRINCE

Your pleading is in vain. I'll grant no mercy,
Nor change his doom. The former judgment stands.
In equity one cannot sentence twice.

CHORUS

Let one ray of your mercy shine at least,
Without impairment of the strictest justice.

PRINCE

Tell us in what respect this thing can be.

CHORUS

This luckless one, betrayed, surprised, and
          captured,
Robbed of the light of day, bound fast with chains
And doomed to toil as Gaza's courts demand,
Feels, in a little while, his strength and flesh

Melted so weak he totters on his bones,
And slowly pines and spends his time in sighs.
Thus pressed upon by dire necessity,
This man, once strong, foresees impending death,
Life's only outcome, and his chief desire.
If, to his comfort, he receives the news
That it is granted him, his suffering done,
To be interr'd in his ancestral tomb,
He would consider this the highest favour.
This is a way to soothe the prisoner's pain
Without the slightest peril to the land.
This boon of tomb and funeral is all
For which he hopes. And you, by granting it,
Shall earn immortal honour, and a name
Among all states, even among your rivals.
Your Highness, grant that women, shy and timid,
And red with shame in voicing their appeal,
May meet with this much favour from you here.
With this our hope, we kneel before your feet,
Low in the dust of earth with reverence.
May "merciful" forever be your title!

PRINCE

Rise, Hebrew maidens. Cease to weep. Be brave,
And wipe away your tears. I'll grant your asking.
I swear by Dagon and his black high altar
That if this Samson dies, none shall withhold
A royal bier, our own court's catafalque,
To bear his body home that he may lie
At peace within his father's sepulchre.
If there be any stronger god by whom
A prince may swear, I call on him to shatter
The vaulted roof of Dagon's house this day
Upon the head of all the Philistines,
And bury and o'erwhelm the revellers!

And if permission lie within your law,
Come, be our midday guests at Dagon's feast!
(*Exit* PRINCE)

CHORUS OF JEWESSES

Strophe I
In junction and partition
The Cosmos moves divine;
God's power keeps the whole at length
Complete in His design
Through unity and balance;
As when a roof with strength
Stress-blended soars yet higher.
What wonder is't that blood to blood
Is drawn in such a fervent flood,
Their veins feel kindred fire!
The child its mother seeks at death
And hails her with its dying breath;
And son seeks rest by sire.

Antistrophe I
So in the fate that lashes
    Sad Samson in his pain,
It seems that as death hovers low
    His mourning heart is fain
To lie beside his father's ashes,
    And find his comfort so.
He grieves at his delusion—
How in an hour of evil plight
The razor shore away his might;
    Then foes from their seclusion
Fell on a poor defenceless man.
His soul's dark torment then began,
    The pangs of love's confusion.

Strophe II
The patriarchs through reason

In spirit all were led,
As time and epoch gave them grace
    To bury each his dead
With sad procession, at death's season,
    In one last resting place
    At Hebron's dim behesting.
In that long-consecrated earth
Sons lie by those that gave them birth.
    Joseph, at his requesting,
Was in the race's ancient style
Conveyed from Memphis and the Nile.
    And there they all are resting.

Antistrophe II
The prince hath sworn with vigour,
    By Dagon hath he sworn.
'Twere best we seek the captive out
    To tell him, lest forlorn
He faint beneath his sorrow's rigour.
    'Twill make his heart more stout
    Amid his prison's badness;
Hearing that grave and funeral
Are now assured, he will not fall
    To pining in that sadness
Where he in utter dark is hived,
Of human comfort quite deprived.
    He will leap up for gladness.

ACT THREE
(*Enter* PRINCE *and* PRINCESS *of Gaza*)

PRINCESS
    The five triumphant courts now gathered here,
    Each at the height of its magnificence,
    To join the holy sacrificial feast,
    As they were bidden, and to celebrate

To the honour of the gods of Palestine,
Desire greatly that the prisoner,
This Samson, should make sport, to grace the feast,
With skilful acting in a temple show
Before the country's dukes and duchesses.
Thus thou canst win the hearts of all the lords
And Dagon's favour likewise. All the ladies
Unanimously urge this from all sides.
If thou, the Prince, permittest, he today
Will play what we desire by his favour.

PRINCE

The drama has beguiled us more than once
Ere this with masterly pretence of truth
And not unhappily: if inculcating
True virtue blent with pleasure for our lords
And painting, to the life, the way o' the world
Through speaking pictures. Men behold a court
Confused, upset, unruly, overthrown
By the sad death of princes. Then they hear
Of outrage and revengefulness. Men drag
Crowned and anointed monarchs from their thrones.
Passions that burn and move are blended there
Like colours which a needle on a loom
Quaintly portrays; a master dramatist
Can in imaginative tapestry
So well portray that he who contemplates it
Vows 'tis divine eye-music. Here the flower
Of apophthegm in heavenly valleys yields
A fragrance and a perfume past compare,
More pleasing to the gods than frankincense
Upheaved to them in golden bowls and censers.
The drama edifies a state; it brooks
No stain of calumny or idle scorn
On holy or unholy. Each one's fault

Is marked without disclosing any name.
Drama is not despised but by the churl
Whose dull soul follows neither right nor reason.
Surely the drama grants a store of wisdom
Upon the stage of Heliopolis,
By the obelisk of Memphis, and the famed
Egyptians' national dramatic school
Who tread the clouds and spare not cost nor labour
To anatomize Dame Nature, limb by limb.
So have they gathered into one the sum
Of all things knowable, a treasury
Of wisdom garnered up by many ages.
The drama feels no mute embarrassment
If human starlings chatter in disfavour.
All princes take much pleasure in the stage.
Who more than we? 'Tis known to thee, milady.

PRINCESS
Thou dost agree then to the thing we wish?

PRINCE
Believe me, art should triumph here today
If thy proposal had been earlier known.
The time is now too short. The temple banquet
Is all arranged.

PRINCESS   Grant us this happiness.
Then shall we see what still may be worked out.
The role of Samson would control the play.

PRINCE
Another point: the priesthood does not yield
To novelty, being conservative.

PRINCESS
At every court, drama is well received.

PRINCE
Play-acting in a temple, by a Jew?

PRINCESS

    If Dagonist or Jew, what does it matter
    Who plays or where one plays?

PRINCE   Temples, however,

    May not be thus profaned. The priests of Dagon
    Will not allow it, by a Hebrew least of all,
    Who, through his harsh new law, directs his scorn
    Against the old worship of the Philistines.
    But if the lords want plays, the theatre
    Of my own court stands ever open for them.

PRINCESS

    To hurry from the temple and the feast
    Into the court, would be most inconvenient.
    But for all sitting at the god's own dish,
    At wine, while men are merry, and the cup
    Goes gaily round, to gaze upon a stage
    And see how each one bravely plays his part
    In honour of the feast would more than double
    Our joys of table. And if piety
    Be deemed, perhaps, the greatest of all virtues,
    How can one blame those worshippers who burn
    With zeal to thank our god and celebrate
    In sport a day devoted to rejoicing,
    When without any blow or loss of blood
    They shadow forth in drama this great blessing
    That weapons never won in twenty years?

PRINCE

    Thine aim is good, but inexpedient.

PRINCESS

    If the Prince grants it, all the world approves.

PRINCE

    Men differ much in nature and in feeling.

PRINCESS
Can man, the rational, be false to reason?

PRINCE
What reason have most men?

PRINCESS   A modicum.

PRINCE
But how can one assign its certain measure?

PRINCESS
Its measure may be gauged by character.

PRINCE
But even character shows variation.

PRINCESS
How is that shown?

PRINCE   By variance in aim.

PRINCESS
But is not reason natural to man?

PRINCE
'Tis nature's gift, but different in each.

PRINCESS
How then on equal footing can men live?

PRINCE
They cannot, for in rationality
Mankind still differs greatly, head for head.

PRINCESS
Authority would therefore seem required
To govern all men with a common judgment.

PRINCE
Men are a race of half-beasts and of whole.
The gods have made this difference innate.
The wisdom of the world has therefore forged

A wise law from necessity, to curb
Those wills that wander from a middle line.
Yet can they, by no means, attain their aim
Through hope of due reward and fear invoked
Of punishment for evil. Hence, indeed,
It is required the curb should go still further:
For secular authority controls
The body, but can never plumb the heart.
Hence came the fear of gods (a higher Power
That knows the thoughts of each, and, like a sword,
Pierces the human bosom mightily,
Troubles the guilty conscience, yet assigns
Peace to the pious, and can estimate,
Within a man, each human soul's deserts)
For the support of states and governments
Through introducing worship, to our good.
The prayerbook and the sword, with like constraint,
Both serve to rule mankind harmoniously.
There is a need for this two-handed Power
Beneath which common men live happily.
The two authorities are harmonized
Like strings upon one note. 'Tis therefore good
That we avoid the discord of a play,
Whose nature might offend this holy feast.
'Tis past the right of secular decree.
In such a case, the head of Dagon's church,
To whom the honour of the deity
Has been committed and who everywhere,
From Gaza ev'n to Dor, from his high throne
Keeps watch above all temples, should be deem'd
The ultimate, august authority.
Men may not use the threshold of God's house
Without the approval of the Holy See.
The high priest can permit it. It is time

A messenger were sent, who should enquire
Whether thy plan would meet with his approval.
What we don't ask will never gain assent.
But I must go. They await me at the court.
(*Exit* PRINCE. *The* PRINCESS *claps her hands and*
A STEWARD *enters*)

PRINCESS
Steward, I wish His Holiness might hear
With favour our immediate request.
Go hence.
(*Exit* STEWARD)
Yet I am loath to trouble him
Amid his priestly business, for no doubt
The ceremonial of worship calls
For his continual care. He has his voice
Of papal jurisdiction to extend,
Backed by his holy seal, so that no priest
May wander from his practice and his rule.
But lo, the high priest even now is coming
Out of the temple gates to speak with us.
(*Enter* HIGH PRIEST)

HIGH PRIEST
Most gracious Princess, may our God preserve thee!

PRINCESS
Most venerable Father, who dost guard
Continually the honour of the gods
And with the bridle of thy laws dost rule
So many folk along Philistia's coast,
The gods have yielded to our hands this foe
Through the power of thy prayers. Now all the lords
Desire that Samson, 'mid the banqueters,
Our foe, but late invincible in strength,
Might in the temple, in a drama, play

A show of victory to Dagon's glory
And to the pleasure of the multitude.
If this plan pleases thee, it pleases us.

HIGH PRIEST

Drama of old found favour with the gods.
Thus was their high name honoured; majesty
Was given to themes that, notably arranged,
Did wondrously delight the auditors.
For when the cast retired at the close,
There then arose the crash of clapping hands,
Lauding the gods, and laughter pealing loud
Forth from the theatre and echoing
O'er wall and water, marketplace and court,
In lingering tumult all along the coast.
Are the lords and ladies eager now for plays?
In that they follow customs and old laws.
Let Samson be apparelled for his part.
Open the theatre. We bless this play
To the resounding praise of Dagon's name.

PRINCESS

The Prince has offered us his theatre
For Samson's acting; but the folk of court
All wish to have it shown within the temple.

HIGH PRIEST

There stands no stage.

PRINCESS   We'll rear one up directly.

The court has carpenters and tools on hand.
Our master carpenter has ample skill
To build the woodwork of a stage at once
Without disturbance to the temple priests.
Likewise the temple minstrels, who perform
So many holy rites, and in such service
Spare neither dress nor instrument of music
But lend their tools and costumes readily,

Shall, as a profitable sign to God,
Be quick to outfit Samson, if thou bid them.

HIGH PRIEST
But is blind Samson ready for such plays?

PRINCESS
What has the man not played? He wrestled, fenced,
And danced the cuirass dance, ere flattering beauty
Deprived him of the possibility.
The congregation of the Jews stood dumb
As often as he served before the ark
And as a singer, to the harp or flute,
Would cunningly caress the ears of all.
We shall within the temple play a masque,
Where Pleasure lays Strength sleeping on a bed
Of roses; then disarms and leads the hero,
Meeker than any lamb, and teaches him
In his blind love to whisper what she will.
Then does the flattering mistress take revenge
In piety upon him in his blindness
To the service of her god.

HIGH PRIEST   What follows then?

PRINCESS
She puts the golden censer in his hand,
Before he smells its fumes, and by her guile
She sways and helps the blind man offer incense
Before the idol, giving Dagon honour.
Then shall the populace applaud so loud
That the Dead Sea and Jordan's flood, amazed,
Shall pour their waters backward; Shiloh, too,
Livid with fear and ill, shall set her lords
To seek for safety when the Jews' great judge
Shall stain their ark with this supreme disgrace.
The blind man, meanwhile, shall throughout his
     role

In the appointed masque, sing, dance, and play
With thy priests, hand in hand, to fitting tunes.
Then shall the gods, out of the clouds, their throne,
Look down, and, as from seats in theatres,
Share in the pleasure of the throng below.
So shall the glorious worship of the Jews
Receive a frightful blow through Samson's acting.

HIGH PRIEST

I would that all our priests might first endorse this.
They stand on points of conscience, to a straw.

PRINCESS

It shall be published ere they take alarm,
Ere Samson comes from out thy temple chapel,
To tread the temple stage, clad like a prince.

HIGH PRIEST

That's well. But name me now the other player.

PRINCESS

The actress who will play the role of Pleasure
Is named Noëma.

HIGH PRIEST   Is she skilled in drama?

PRINCESS

She is a woman whose transcendent acting
Hath so enthralled our country's richest man
That utterly breft of all his senses
He has pledged his troth to the fickle, faithless
        charmer.

HIGH PRIEST

That's near the life of Samson, should he play;
And to thy mind, the art seems born in him.

PRINCESS

They chose him judge before his twentieth year.
His wisdom then already matched his strength,
And gave him such renown.

HIGH PRIEST   And a flatterer took
    This paragon of wisdom and of strength
    And caught him in the grievous toils of love?

PRINCESS
    Thus do men often err, through love of women.
    'Tis pardonable, especially in the great.

HIGH PRIEST
    Though I distrust all Hebrews, yet my heart
    Is kindled by thy plan. We give consent,
    Since with this drama thou wilt honour Dagon.

PRINCESS
    Thou wilt oblige the lords and this proud port
    Of Gaza by the play.

HIGH PRIEST   It is approved.
    Ho, temple warden, haste! Let the blind man
    Come here to know what is the royal pleasure.
    Give orders that a temple stage be built.
    Provide such curtains, carpets, instruments
    Of music, and costumery as may
    Be of due service to this pious play.
                    (*Exit* HIGH PRIEST)

PRINCESS (*alone*)
    How keen I am that Samson may assent!
    We'll ply him with warm promises and try
    To kindle confidence within his bosom
    That he more willingly may do the pleasure
    Of the courtiers and myself. To soothe his woe
    May serve to lull hostility to sleep.
    He comes. I must beguile this Jew with hopes.
                    (*Enter* SAMSON *and* ATTENDANT)

SAMSON
    Where am I led?

ATTENDANT   Thou com'st before the Princess.

SAMSON
Say rather my most fierce and cruel foe.

ATTENDANT
He who is conquered learns to bear the yoke.

SAMSON
O bitter schooling, beaten black and blue,
Famished and spent with moiling in the mill,
Deprived of heaven's light, and destitute
Of hope and comfort!

ATTENDANT   Rightly, that no Jew
May set our corn on fire with captured foxes.

PRINCESS
Take courage, captive Lord! Thou canst thyself
Gain freedom and deliverance from thy burden.
Be wise! One can win mercy by complaisance.

SAMSON
No man, no prince, can give me back my eyes.
With sight one loses more than half of life.
The day has gone forever. I await
The ruddy flush of dawning nevermore.
Here is eternal night. All other beasts
Sleep in the night and rest, but in this night
Sad Samson sees no rest prepared for him.

PRINCESS
So pitiful thou seem'st, I too am sorry.

SAMSON
See this sick body, how my flesh is wasted!
Behold, my legs already sway and totter.
I change into a shadow. Yet my plea
Serves not to mitigate the warden's rage.
My punishment continues, though my strength
Wanes fast away. Men cry: "Cease not from work!
The court needs flour. Forth, forth to grind, to grind!"

The court reviles me, puts me under guard.
Men ride an ass's neck off in this style!
Is there then no compassion? Ah, man's art
Can soften even a hard diamond;
But though I sweat out blood, no tears can touch
My foes' hard heart that still is obdurate.
If all the flour I grind is not enough,
Then cut me up and stew my wasted body,
Make pottage of my bones. In my mere meat
Is little worth. It stinks, and soon must rot.
Let your mouths taste it, and your maws ferment!
May't prosper you as food. Taste! Taste! For thus
You can announce how Samson, dead from toiling,
And eaten up, lies buried in your bellies.
False love more frightful than a tiger's tooth
Has torn me for its food. Your hate remains.
And now this feast rejoices over Samson.
You mock him. But the spindle of his life
Is running out. His body shrinks apace.
The soul, thus trammelled, seeks an ampler air.
One sob, and then no more. One final sigh.

PRINCESS

Brave hero, calm thyself. All this vexation
And wild lament can only gall and pain thee.
We have desired (pray credit this to one
Thou hast called foe!) to advise thee in thy plight,
And, if we do not free thee, at the least
To lighten thy sad lot. If thou approve,
We shall make haste to give abundant proof.

SAMSON

And is milady pleased, on Dagon's day,
Thus rudely to make mockery of a slave,
One in thy power, a poor blind prisoner
With death impending, yea, and more than death?

My sighs, my yearning sobs by night and day,
Are all for a quick death, a thousand deaths.
O God, thou seest and dost know my need!

PRINCESS

If thou couldst trust me, I would do my best.

SAMSON

Believe me, all my thought is set on death.

PRINCESS

No, no! One doesn't die thus! Though thy state
Is grievous, yet a too tenacious bond
Holds soul and body coupled. All too strong
Is spun the fabric of the web of life.
'Tis seen in all that dying men endure
Before that web's unravelled. Some there are
Who find it passing hard to make an end.

SAMSON

How dost thou think to mitigate my lot?
Dare Samson hope that he may grind no more?
Canst thou distinguish between slaves and princes?

PRINCESS

Here is my hand to promise thee relief.

SAMSON

O hand, how long hast thou delayed this hour!

PRINCESS

Henceforth, thou'lt toil no longer in the mill.

SAMSON

What is it now that can awaken favour,
And gain it from the Prince?

PRINCESS   This solemn feast
Requires something mutual. We do know
That thou art gifted with the arts of fence,
Of wrestling and of leaping. Samson has,

They say, great skill in dancing and in singing,
Likewise in drama; for the princely Moses
Invoked the artistic wisdom of the Nile
And bade his Hebrews cultivate this art.
If thou couldst condescend to grace our triumph
By acting in a stage Morality
In Dagon's temple, where our lords are gathered,
We shall relieve the yoke that galls thy neck.

SAMSON

If I, with acting and with song, can win
My freedom, in this hope I'll undertake
A holy drama that the Philistines
Will carry in remembrance evermore.

PRINCESS

In Dagon's temple at the feast thou'lt gladden
The hearts of thousands.

SAMSON   Will they suffer it?

PRINCESS

We have, with trouble, won the High Priest over.
He has approved; and now they seek an actress
Who at the feast may act a role that blends
As complement with thine, Noëma named,
A woman richly dowered by art and nature.

SAMSON

Let her invent the play, a moral masque
That teaches one to curb a wanton nature.
Together we'll rehearse and fashion it;
And I with song and dance and heavenly music
Shall, as with noble juices, season so
The courses of the drama that thereafter
Nothing shall ever vex my audience.
Though I shall gain but little thanks at Shiloh,
I seek deliverance from my disaster.
Against that aim, what reason should contend?

PRINCESS

> Go hence in peace. Have thyself richly clothed.
> Be not afraid amid the crowd to walk,
> Before the sacred throng. Then wait a while
> In the chapel of our temple till the hour
> They call thee forth to play the destined play
> According to the plans agreed upon.

SAMSON

> The right way to gain freedom from these fetters.

PRINCESS (*to* ATTENDANT)

> Escort this prince of Israel to the chapel,
> And clothe him there according to his rank.
> Change thy clothes likewise there, and hold thee
>   ready.
>   (*Exit* SAMSON *and* ATTENDANT)
> How quickly the Jew changed when he was told
> Of his relief. The hope of freedom lured him.
> The splendid concourse here, the temple triumph,
> And the fierce fame of Samson's play and incense
> Shall raise the gods of Gaza to the sky
> And so cast down and fright the pallid Hebrews
> That in our palace here this embassy
> Shall rest perforce in the most abject peace.
>   (*Exit* PRINCESS)

CHORUS OF JEWESSES

> *Strophe I*
> If blindness of the body's vision
>   A grave impairment must imply;
> A greater loss were the elision
>   Of seeing from the inward eye,
> If souls be valued at true worth.
> The body is but dust and earth,
>   A spirit-essence is the soul.
> The body is in Time, decaying;
> The soul is deathless, still obeying

The purpose of a vaster whole:
Fervent it seeks beyond the humble clod
The source of all just spirits, even God.

Antistrophe I
Blind, captive Samson here is surer
  How bad the loss of eyes can be,
And yet the Philistines are poorer
  Amid their land's prosperity:
  For they have lost their inward sight
  Yet do not know they walk in night.
    They lack the eye of true desire—
That knows the God of light unending,
And on Him in true faith depending,
  Is thrilled by heaven's holy fire.
Sight to the humblest brute of earth is given,
But reason teaches us to soar towards heaven.

Strophe II
If all their blindness of unreason
  Were known to the uncircumcized,
Would they praise Dagon in his season,
  By cunning arts of hell surprised?
Would they with gifts from west and east
Make merry at the temple feast,
  Forsaking Him who made each one,
  Whose all-creative arm enfolds them?
  Alas, the night of Dagon holds them:
  They lose far more than any sun,
Even the one true Nature never swerving,
Light of the Godhead, ever praise-deserving!

Antistrophe II
Us Jews a fairer fate engages:
  The radiance of the great I AM
Was first revealed in bygone ages
  To our forefather Abraham.
And later still He showed His cause

To Moses in His holy laws.
When many gods of one are born
 False idols are the lie's abettors.
  Jehovah, guard thou in his fetters
  Heroic Samson, mocked to scorn
By Dagon's servants in their impudence!
Thou art alone his strength and his defence.

ACT FOUR

(*Enter* ATTENDANT)

ATTENDANT

The Jewish judge, condemned by Gaza's justice,
And doomed to contumely and disgrace,
Begins to fear, as he before the priests
In Dagon's congregation shall be led
Through all the press and throng. Now must he tread
The temple stage, before the temple feast,
Dressed in his own true character of Strength
Caught in the snare of Pleasure, and by her
Bereft of sight and chained in endless darkness,
A slave men break by toil. Now shall he beg
For freedom, offering incense at the altar.
This irks his body and his blood is seething
With hatred and revenge, but all in vain.
His hair, the brood-nest of his mighty strength,
Is shorn away, and he but feebly walks.
Go, fetch him. See he comes, and gasps for breath,
And seems to doubt the freedom promised him.
He bellows, foams at mouth, and grinds his teeth.
His eyebrows brood revenge and bristle horrors.
Vengeance begins to kindle, and he stamps,
Tosses his head and cannot speak for rage.
The lion-taming, land-despoiling Jew,
Unlike himself, dares rend no lion now,

Tearing it by the muzzle, ears, and tail;
No land can he molest with fiery foxes,
Till flaming wheat is all the eye can see.
The poor inhabitants, deprived of harvest,
Lamented so a heart of stone might break;
But he sat laughing coolly on a hill-top,
Exulting in their woes. O firebrand!
But soft: I had best be silent, ere he hear;
Best listen on one side while he complains
And talks, but all untimely, of revenge.

(*Enter* SAMSON)

SAMSON

O God of Abraham look down!
Behold my wretched case at length,
And grant again my former strength!
What shame bemocks Thy name's renown
Among these blind idolaters,
These Philistines that flout thy law
With Dagon's insolent guffaw!
This, more than all, my suffering stirs.
I have o'ercome my blind distress.
Now make me, if Thou wilt, more strong!
To Thee my zealous thoughts belong;
Thee only would my heart address.
Thine honour, Father in the skies,
Is all my race has ever sought;
So Abraham, the unvanquished, thought;
Thine honour doth transcend mine eyes.
To lead me round the knaves now come;
My seven curls they fasten too;
With staves they'll beat my body blue
Before their god, to fife and drum.
They can exult with mocking voice
Above poor Samson, spent and blind;
So long as he no strength can find,

Let ruthless Palestine rejoice.
But here amid the heathens' feast
Omnipotence will soon be found
To be in hair by no means bound,
Nor sadly, in its shearing, ceased.
My angel Fadaël today
Came to console me where I knelt,
Praying to God that strength be dealt.
And lo, new strength within me lay!
That God that from my mother's womb
Has marked me out for deeds immense,
Now bids me strive with confidence
And promises a princely tomb,
Compared with which no pyramid
At Memphis reared so high in air
And widely famous everywhere
Shall my memorial outbid.
No jawbone, as God strengthens me,
Nor giants slain nor cornfields burned
Nor Gaza's gate shall seem to have earned
Fierce triumph o'er God's enemy!

ATTENDANT

Illustrious prince, I hear thy sad laments.
Towards thee I've borne myself, at the command
Of our good duchess, as thy rank requires.
Men, with respect, have brought thee princely
          garments.
Rich robes of state, and, for thy lofty head,
That thou mayst shine before the eyes of all,
A sumptuous turban with a nodding plume,
Buckled by diamonds. Why therefore grieve,
Dwelling upon the curse of captive shame,
As if thy heart were pregnant with revenge?
Thou art deprived of sight—'Tis sad, and true.
No lord, no prince, no king in all this life

Can give thee back thine eyes; yet Dagon can,
The god in whom this capital believes,
God of our oath and honour. Ay, my Lord,
Shake not thy head in wrath. I do but speak
After the style and usage of our land,
For worship brings this also in the realms.
If thou couldst let thyself be reconciled
To all the faith and practice of our priests
Thou wouldst win mighty honour here in Gaza
And love among our people, till at last
Thou sattest in Philistia's judgment-seat
With far more honour than in Israel's towns.

SAMSON (*aside*)

A youth braves Samson with impunity!
That suffered he from no young lion, who,
Frantic with hunger, roaring from his den,
Came leaping to attack with open mouth.
Oh, for an ass's jawbone or a cudgel!
These giants of the shore have need of weapons.
None bears Sir Samson, but these arms of mine
Are stronger once again than steel or stone.
I am the man I was. These are the claws
Never provoked without incurring vengeance
Along Philistia's shores and mountain-heights.
No guard shall long, God willing, snarl at me.
My strength, that in its weakness ground their corn,
If but once more it may repeat its power,
Shall grind a grist of skulls and human bones
And so regard the past as richly paid for.
My feet still firmer than two pillars stand,
The thunder-smitten posts of Dagon's temple.
Why stayest thou thy vengeance? Wait no more!
Burst forth, burst forth! 'Tis time to show thyself.
How my blood seethes, compressed and purulent!
Dark tides of gall are coursing through my veins.

Reclaim, reclaim thine eyes from those who stole them!
Endure no more this mockery and scorn!
As the long brooding fires of a storm
Break forth at last from out a pregnant cloud,
Making the pallid people faint and fear,
Bombarded by fierce bolt and lightning flash,
That strike at everything that rears its crown
In arrogance to flout the Deity,
Whose lightnings have no weak regard for towers
Nor battlement, nor temple, stone nor hill;
So shall my vengeance, mocked and trapped, at last,
Though seeming now to slumber in a grave,
Rise, to the ruin of the Dagonists,
So that this land may cry to God in pain.
My hair, that hung about my neck, and curled
About my forehead like a crown of gold,
I shake, alas, no longer when I shout,
Nor know my power hidden safe within it.
I thrust my thumbs first, therefore, in these sockets,
Whose eyes have been so cruelly bored out,
And call for vengeance ere I die the death.
What vengeance? Surely God's, enjoined on me.
Then call I upon God, my God, for strength.
My God, look earthward from the arch of heaven!
What do I ask? My eyes, from these my foes.—
There came an answering thunderbolt so fierce
It seemed the trembling earth would pass away
When smitten such a blow! And how shall I,
A blind and feeble man, make boast of strength?
My hand is childish to the hand of God!

ATTENDANT

I would thou gavest glory to our Dagon,
A deity who could enhance thy strength.

SAMSON

Silence, lad, silence! Cease to blaspheme God!
We will not alter or degenerate

From Moses' way, however much thou ravest.
Lead me, I pray thee, to thine idol's chapel.
We shall, I promise thee, display God's power
When Dagon's temple tumbles down in pieces.

ATTENDANT

If Dagon's temple shall fall down today,
Forsooth thy head will reel with such a blow.
(*Exit* SAMSON *and* ATTENDANT. *Enter* HIGH PRIEST)

HIGH PRIEST

The Sibyl of high Akkaron, conveyed
In her horse-litter, from reports I hear,
Is greatly moved lest dust of disrepute
May fall today upon the Dagonists.
Let Dagon's court be ready! Go, my men!
I have a hundred sacrificial oxen
All duly dedicated. Altar fires
Are laid and kindled. Every priest of mine
Is busy. If this venerable nun
Disturbs the congregation, what indeed
Are we to do? This irks me to the bone,
Worn as I am with age. The holy care
Of this and all the sea-towns is entrusted
To mine episcopacy, that the Jews
May brew no violence, to wreck our altars.
Help, then, O Dagon! Wherefore shouldst thou lose
All sacrifice and honour? Shall these upstarts,
With Moses' book in one hand and a sword
Held in the other, ravage this our coast
Victoriously, against all right and reason?
Here comes the grey old nun, and as she walks
A girl on either side supports her gently.
            (*Enter* SIBYL *of Akkaron*)
Most worthy lady, dost thou likewise come
To join our festival? Thrice welcome, then,
With thy pure train of consecrated nuns!

SIBYL

We have come here in haste from Akkaron.
Father, I thought to find thee in the temple;
Not in these streets. May God increase thy zeal!

HIGH PRIEST

Mother, what zeal has brought thee here today,
To the great feast? Surely thou hast due reason!

SIBYL

Well to the purpose. We should not have come
For light cause to disturb thee in the midst
Of thy pure duties and the ceremonies
That honour here the holy name of Dagon.
O sanctuary, temple, altars, choirs!
O pious worshippers, unnumbered souls
Here gathered for this triumph of the god!
What dark clouds see we hanging over Gaza!

HIGH PRIEST

Tell what thou seest. We shall listen gladly.

SIBYL

The Prince of Gaza purposed with his Princess
To venture hither. Thronged with courtiers
And nobles, men prepared an offering
To send the concourse forth with holy prayers:
But all that met us in the gods' high service
Was dark with evil omen. Altar flames,
Blood-red, refused to rise. There were defects
In all the beasts: The entrails were quite blue,
With clots of blood. The tallow would not burn.
The liver was decayed. All augurs stood
In mute amazement, looking on each sign
With weeping eyes. The fane was full of hauntings:
The cries of men and women, and the crash
Of buildings tottering. The temple pillars
Were seen to shudder. Then a voice was heard,

Late in the evening, and the temple echo
Answered it seven times from shrine and chancel.
It seemed to say: "Alas, now all is lost!"
The steeple likewise spoke; the copper door
Woke to hoarse clanging, struck by no man's hand.
The augurs saw a serpent on the road
Attack a highwayman most furiously,
Its tooth fast in his heel until he died.
The astrologers, so wise in lore, beheld
The starry Giant rout a host in heaven.
The priesthood, in amazement, mourned and
     muttered,
And to my sanctuary came for counsel.
At their request, I piously put on
My consecrated surplice, crowned my brow
With laurel as a devotee of God,
Then decked it with a snow-white veil of silk,
And fell down in the chancel on my face
And thrice besought the Deity: "O God,
If we present thee with our offerings,
And honour thee with prayers, and thou dost grant
Thine answer to the hearts that ask of thee,
Vouchsafe in our bewilderment today
A revelation of the dark disaster
Foretold by these unholy auspices!
Protect thy temple from untimely fate,
And warn us of the hour that we should shun!"
Then at that prayer the chancel sighed and moaned,
As when a pregnant woman sits dismayed
In agony of childbirth. On my face
I waited prostrate, listening for a voice.
At last these words came bursting from the shrine:
"The Jewish tragedy shall all remember!"
We cried: "May God protect the Prince and Princess!"
And all who heard were mazed in mind and heart.

The priests to Gaza brought us. On the way
The rumour met our ears on every side
That Samson is to act in Dagon's temple.

HIGH PRIEST

Is this thy trouble? Here no ruin lies.

SIBYL

If no calamity were due from this,
Surely the oracle had left us sleeping.

HIGH PRIEST

We praise the holy oracles of God
And his interpreter.

SIBYL   Whene'er they serve thee,
Accept their warning, for the people's sake.

HIGH PRIEST

Believe me, there is nothing here to shun.

SIBYL

'Tis manifest God's warnings then concern thee.

HIGH PRIEST

How does God warn? I would have clear instruction.

SIBYL

He warns thee that this play shall turn out ill.

HIGH PRIEST

Repeat the oracle once more, I pray.

SIBYL

"The Jewish tragedy shall all remember!"

HIGH PRIEST

That statement surely threatens no disaster.

SIBYL

It means the play will bring calamity.

HIGH PRIEST

It means men will remember it with joy.

SIBYL
>If thou wilt thus interpret, I resign.

HIGH PRIEST
>We do not recklessly oppose thy rights.

SIBYL
>Then listen to God's mouthpiece, and be safe.

HIGH PRIEST
>This ambiguity gives scope for choice.

SIBYL
>The choice bears hope to win or pain to lose.
>'Tis safer that ye trust the chancel nun,
>To whom God's spirit has revealed the meaning.

HIGH PRIEST
>I pray thee, let us treat this theme with reason.

SIBYL
>Agreed. From reason we have naught to fear.

HIGH PRIEST
>What guilty act would bring such punishment?

SIBYL
>To desecrate the temple with a Jew.

HIGH PRIEST
>Instead of wrong, this play shall honour Dagon.

SIBYL
>The Jewish play profanes God's house and God.

HIGH PRIEST
>The lords themselves, as drama lovers, urge it.

SIBYL
>The laity are blind to holy things.

HIGH PRIEST
>Pure Dagonists, and true to Ashtaroth.

SIBYL

Dost thou flout God and foster temple quarrels?

HIGH PRIEST

We've often sent to Akkaron for counsel.

SIBYL

God's mouth now answers, and her word is scorned.

HIGH PRIEST

Men must have daily converse with the Jews.

SIBYL

We are divinely bidden to avoid them.

HIGH PRIEST

Dost thou so strictly urge it for a play?

SIBYL

They shatter temples, hew down temple groves,
And burn the images of those high gods
Who burn our land; and then in exultation
They dare to warm themselves beside the embers.

HIGH PRIEST

If their judge plays before great Dagon's altar
And waves the golden censer to his image,
There shall be wailing before Shiloh's ark
And all the envious Hebrews shall be humbled.

SIBYL

Thou seekest for thy course a specious colour.
Beware! One shall not see from any tower
All the misfortune that shall sprout from this.

HIGH PRIEST

What should I do? Why halt, and make an end?
This play has been endorsed by our free will.
They asked our counsel. Shall we rouse disputes
And bring down on our neck the sore displeasure
Of lords and ladies? That were past repair.

Shall we revoke our solemn ordinance
Because of an ambiguous oracle?

SIBYL

Just as thou wilt. Beware! Beware, I say!
Follow thy pleasure. We have done our duty.
Thou art possessed by Jewry's evil spirit.
Their firebrand shall, at a temple-play,
Mock in his heart the sacraments of God.
A brothel pleased him more than Dagon's temple
In times gone by. He never set a foot
Across our sacred thresholds. Surely now
We know these Hebrews, circumcized in body
But not in spirit, care not for religion
Beyond the laws that Pharaoh's foundling founded;
And thus they injure all old laws, and drive
True princes from their lands with fire and sword.
Had Samson been dispatched when fast asleep
In the lascivious bed and burning bosom
Of his false mistress, smothered in his dream,
He would not now be destined here to deal
The realm of Palestine so dire a blow
That it will never pass from man's remembrance.

HIGH PRIEST

This from a blind man, mild as a young lamb?
If thou hadst heard his legs, his sapless bones,
Weary with milling, rattle as he walked,
Thou wouldst not groundlessly proclaim that ruin
Would come from such a man upon our country.

SIBYL

From him 'twill come, if we may trust our God.
It is my right to explain the oracle,
And the whole priesthood would declare me true.

HIGH PRIEST

Art thou infallible in wit and judgment?

SIBYL

Wouldst thou dismiss and carp at oracles?

HIGH PRIEST

In no wise. (*aside*) Who can still this thunderstorm?
(*aloud*) Madam, thou hast arrived here all too late.
When one can speak betimes, with counsel due,
In an assembly of our general priesthood,
Objections yield before authority
And dubious issues find mature decisions.

SIBYL

We came at once, as God inspired us.
And if thou dost not let thyself be stirred
By all these many portents, thou'rt condemned
By all divine and human elements.

HIGH PRIEST

This triumph of our nation must proceed
Even if talk of omens has been heard.

SIBYL

This drama must be stopped.

HIGH PRIEST   Nay, that offends
The high decree that we have firmly pledged.
For neither voice nor ghost nor haruspex,
Rumour nor augur nor astrologer,
Nor palmist's dream nor nunnish intuition
Shall I confound mine own authority.
On any other ground, I'd yield to thee.

SIBYL

In Akkaron, before the temple chapter,
We'll testify that we have done our duty
To ward off this disaster that impends
With hoarse reverberations through the land.
O grievous times to come! God's oracle
Is given us in vain when men dispute it.

Thus they reject God's worship. Thus the church
Has no interpreter. The Deity
Sits mute indeed. And all our pious folk
Who seek for counsel shall, with altered hope,
Hasten to ask advice from Shiloh's shrine.
Thus will the Hebrew's god be reverenced.

HIGH PRIEST

Thine oracle is not opposed here now,
But only found to bear a gentler meaning.
We differ only in interpretation.

SIBYL (*to* ATTENDANT)

Prepare my coach! 'Tis high time we departed!

HIGH PRIEST

I pray thee, grace the concourse with thy presence.

SIBYL

Prepare my coach! Away! We stay too long.
Trust me, some plague shall fall without delay.
Here no wise counsel carries weight. Belike
The theatre, along with Dagon's temple
And all that cleave to this abomination
Nor heed at all my prophecy and warning,
Shall fall and perish in calamity.

HIGH PRIEST

Excuse us, madam. We are pressed for time.
The priests watch busily. The festival
Summons us now within. And Samson, clothed
For his due part, stands ready and prepared
To follow the attendant who shall lead him.
        (*Exit* SIBYL. *Enter* CHORISTERS *of Dagon*)

HIGH PRIEST

        How the ceremonial throng,
        Notable for play and song,
        Enters in the name of Dagon,

By whose might is our dismay gone.
Let Philistia's soldiers come,
Marching here to fife and drum,
Holy horn and trumpet festal.
Let God's clergy, priest and vestal,
Walk in order, two and two,
Crowned with oak leaves as their due,
Stepping with deportment stately,
Honouring the feast sedately.
Let the chorus, chanting free,
Blend with harp and psaltery;
Samson marching to these choirs
Boasts a handsome band of squires.
Then the torch; the censer then;
Dagon's image, praised of men,
Borne enthroned, is bright with treasure.
Prompt are we to do his pleasure.
Follow him, in such a band,
All the nobles of the land,
All the great ones and their ladies,
Splendid as the court of Hades.
Sing ye choristers, for us!
Speed the blest procession thus!

CHORISTERS

Great is Dagon, great past doubting,
He who gave into our power
God's great foe in startled hour,
Him who smote, the giants routing,
Him who in himself was strong,
Without sword or war's fierce chattel,
 As a host arrayed for battle,
Marching terribly along.
Great is Dagon, great past doubting,
Who in bonds has set God's foe,
In our hands has brought him low

To the blind Jew's utter flouting,
He by whom the Philistines
Ever in the field were beaten.
Dagon's hands our cup did sweeten:
See, at last proud Gaza wins!
Great is Dagon, great past doubting,
Who hath tumbled to his fall
God's great foe, once feared by all,
Comrades, lift your hearts with shouting!
At the banquet all shall see
Samson acting, like a master,
Acting out his own disaster.
Fear not, though he roar at thee!
                    (*Exeunt*)

CHORUS OF JEWESSES

> *Strophe*
> When the sun scatters, at his setting,
>   His rays upon the human race
>   From out the lion's heavenly space,
> The lion, greater strength begetting,
>   Becomes in heat too stark:
>   As in the wild-beast park
>   The king of furry creatures,
>   Most grim and fierce in features,
>   With muscles, teeth, and claws,
>   Devours and overawes.
> The sun, with lion's blood replete,
> Makes all things yield before its heat.
>
> *Antistrophe*
> So here may Gaza meet with anguish
>   An end of racial war at length
>   If God shall give our hero strength,
> Samson, who, dying, seems to languish.
>   Men caught him unaware

And sheared his long, fierce hair;
But God is never bounded
By hair or things confounded;
  Working through heroes still,
  He strengthens whom He will.
Though for a time His hand He stays,
He always vindicates His ways.

Epode
If Samson may confirm God's time
By doing here a deed sublime
And wake the land to endless woe,
The sun shall from the lion glow.
The Philistines and all they cherish
Shall melt away and seem to perish:
Thus melts God's sun a mount of snow.

ACT FIVE

CHORUS
Mercy, O God, have mercy! Help us now!
Comfort us in this need! We cry from earth
To Thy high throne. Oh, what a crash was that!
Alas, where are we? That terrific fall
Deafens our ears. This dust makes blind our eyes.
We choke. We die with dust. This rubbish, flying
Dustily through the city, fills the air.
The great metropolis is full of shrieks.
The sound of howling and of groaning spreads.
The city sits forsaken, overwhelmed
In grief. Each seeks his dead, and knows not yet
Th' extent of the disaster. It were best
That we, perhaps, look not about for news.
We'll hide for a little in this temple hedge.
Here comes a man, amazed and stupefied.
Now let us ask, and learn how things have gone.
          (*Enter* MESSENGER)

Ho, courtier! Prithee, pause a moment here,
And tell us what has happened.

MESSENGER   Hebrew damsels,
Alas, all Gaza's lost. In ruin lies
All this fair country of the Philistines.

CHORUS
But what of Samson? Is he dead or living?

MESSENGER
Stone dead. I would he had been slain long since
Instead of being blinded, chained, maltreated,
And led about, hardened in bitterness!
He has involved himself in his revenge.

CHORUS
So do we Hebrews lose our judge and guardian.
That is most sad. But tell us, point by point,
All thou hast heard and seen.

MESSENGER   I saw revenge
At which the world is moved. The Sibyl knew
As clearly in foreboding what would happen
As if she had seen Dagon's temple fall.
This comes of playing dramas in God's church,
Profaned thus by a Jew, alone too strong
For all our country. We saw Samson first
Conducted to the gathering; he walked
Before the sanctuary to the tune
Of pipes and strings and songs of victory
And happy festal lays. He stood with patience
Through all the scorns and mockings of the folk;
Meek as a lamb, he held himself in check
But ruminated upon secret grudges.
Thus came the rites of Dagon to their end.
The sacrificial meal, as men are wont,
Was next begun, beyond all precedent

In splendour, out of joy that by the nose
They led their greatest foe, distressed and blind,
A prisoner. Men gave him honeycomb
And taunted him to test if it were sweet
As that wild honey of the bees that swarmed
In the young lion's carcass rent by him
In his full strength of old, before he dreamt
Of taking part in Gaza's temple banquets.
They asked him if the uncertainty of riddles
Did not occur to him: Who now seemed strongest?
Was not an army stronger than one man?
The priests then crowned his head with oak-leaf
        chaplets,
With invitation to their guest to dance
In front of Dagon's altar. He stood mute,
As one both deaf and dumb. A toast went round
To Samson's judgeship, drunk with great guffaws.
They wished him luck, another pair of eyes.
The mockery had no end. At last there came
A woman forth, Noëma, to conclude
The meal with no unedifying drama,
But a fine moral masque, to match the day.
They stepped upon the stage and set to work.
First sang he to the harp, a merry song
In keeping with the play, a lilting air.
The company rejoiced; they laughed aloud.
The temple echoed with their jocund cries,
Their joy in wine, as the great cup went round
In praise of Dagon and his fellow gods.
As the feast closed, the play was to begin.
Blind Samson said: "Lad, lead me now, I pray,
Where the stage leans against the two chief pillars
That bear the frightful mass of all the temple,
For we would rest, exhausted by our sport,
And then begin once more with strength refreshed

Before the eyes of all. To pause awhile
Strengthens the spirit with reviving breath."
He, conscious of his dark revengeful plan
That all too soon would burst forth into light
And work the ruin of Philistia's lords,
Handled on either side the massy pillars
That bore the temple, crowded with its thousands,
A mighty masterpiece of giants' hands:
Down through the upper roof spectators gazed:
Thousands in high successive galleries,
Three tiered, sat row on row; while underneath
A countless throng in chancel, nave, and aisles
Strained anxiously to see the play by Samson.
It seems that he suspected how Noëma
Would treacherously deceive him in the play
When, as he held the censer, she would lead him,
In his stark blindness, to the throne of Dagon,
And he, with her, would wave the incense there
To the gross mockery of Aaron's service,
At which the lords of proud Philistia
Would terminate the feast with wild applause.
But it went otherwise: that comedy
Before the great came to a tragic end
And finished in a gust of utter terror.

CHORUS

We dread that tragic end as it approaches.

MESSENGER

He stood between the pillars, burning fierce
With an exalted soul, a power divine,
Strength greater than that lately taken from him.
Distorting his blind brows, he gnashed his teeth
And seemed like some proud lion, who, once bound
And with fresh wounds uncured, tosses his head,
Tears loose the galling ropes that held him captive,

And roars so terribly that all who hear
Hold themselves lost. The hair on Samson's head
Seemed suddenly to grow. He raised his face,
Fronting the vault of heaven, and cried aloud:
"My God, my God, come down and walk below!
Protect Thy name now, and reclaim mine eyes!
Now is the time to show Thy strength in me!"
Then tugged he cross-wise at the two chief pillars
With both his arms, so that they bent, and cried:
"Die now, my soul, with all the Philistines!"
Then as the cramp irons yielded suddenly,
The rafters, roof, and galleries gave way,
Robbed of the proud support that held aloft
The mighty weight of building and of men.
Death-shrieks arise, and groans of the half-dead,
Amid thick clouds of wreckage and of dust.
The earth's foundation trembles with the blow;
The sound goes forth, and spreads by hill and dale.
All Gaza thinks of flight, and from the hills
The giants, proud at the great feast, look forth
And sink in spirit, low as Dagon fell,
Buried beneath the wreckage with the dead,
Where one grave has engulfed both high and low.
Philistia, that had reared its head to heaven,
Has now received more dire a blow from Samson
Then all its routs in all its history.
And here they lie together in their death:
The avenger, mad with grief at his distress,
Took with him all his foes by utter force.

CHORUS
Lucky thou art, to escape to tell of it.

MESSENGER
I clung upon a pillar at one side
That leaned but did not fall, and so I saw

All of this piteous drama from above.
When by degrees the dust-clouds disappeared,
Amid the ruins, red with oozing blood,
Were men and women, crushed or partly crushed,
Broken in neck, splintered in every bone,
Dead, or just gasping forth a choking ghost.
One tried to pull away a mangled arm:
Another staggered groaning from the wreck
Where legs and heads and entrails merged and
          mixed
In a disgusting batter: bone with flesh
And pulp of brain defiled pollute the day
With reek that soon will bring a pestilence.
Hither from all sides anxious citizens
Rush to locate their kindred and their friends
And search the bloody wreckage through and
          through.
The corpses, crushed and dusty, are not plain
Even to the scanning of familiar eyes.
The way they wring their hands and groan and
          shriek
Is past enduring. When the face is crushed,
In whole or part, they know them by their clothes,
Or seek for birth-marks on the mangled flesh,
Or judge them by the years and sex of each.

CHORUS
      Didst thou not see or know what happened Samson?

MESSENGER
      A heavy stone, I gather, crushed his heart
      And put it out of misery. Men have set
      The body on a bier, out of respect
      For you, the Hebrews. For in dire bereavement
      The city finds it inexpedient
      To stir up hosts of lions over one.

They know the Prince had pledged his funeral,
So bring the litter here without delay.
Ye might, an't please you, take the body out
From the court's postern gate, and so avoid
The troubled high street and the noise of folk
Just overwhelmed and seething in their hate.
        (*Enter* RELATIVES *of Samson*)

RELATIVES

We had hoped to see the hero ere he died.
But is not this a band of Hebrew women?

CHORUS

Timely ye come and meet us here, to escort
With your due grief the funeral of your blood.
There comes the bier. Sit down a little space,
In the churchyard, by this hedge. The Governor
Returns, alas, in very different guise
From when he lately sallied forth to wrest
Red plunder from the hands of infidels.
We had come here that we might speak to him,
But hearing how devoutly he has fought
To free himself with such a rare revenge,
We come instead to the burial of his body.
Now let us all set forth! May God protect
The body and ourselves, while all the folk
In Gaza give themselves to lamentation.
        (*Enter* FADAËL)

FADAËL

Ye sons and daughters of the patriarch,
Great Abraham, be not afraid! I come
On your account, down from the gate of heaven.
I am the angel Fadaël, who foretold
To Samson's parents his miraculous birth,
How that the barren should yet bear a son

Promised to heaven from his mother's womb;
How razor ne'er might desecrate his hair
Nor wine his tongue; for he should greatly free
His native land from the Philistian power.
Now has the steadfast hero carried out
God's vengeance, through his zeal for God's own
    cause.
Let not his death distress you; for his spirit,
Freed from the body's blindness and all care,
Is now at last in peace in the cool shade
Beside the ancient heroes of his race
Who likewise walked in valour in their day.
After twelve hundred years, he shall be led
Through all the stars on high, and there shall see
A type of his own fame enthroned on high,
Drawn on a chariot among God's saints
In triumph, and then clearly understand
That the example of his death and life
Foretells a Saviour, of God's spirit born,
Who shall be persecuted, as was he,
And dying, deal a fatal blow to death;
But through a softer law He shall unburden
Each heart of its revenge—a law of love
That puts the highest crown on human life.
Ye shall build splendidly the hero's tomb
Beside his father's body, and shall cause
This writing to be carved upon the stone:
"Here lies the hero Samson, who could guard
The people of his God. What hero? He
Who vanquished, in his death, the Philistines."
Stand up, and follow straightway with this bier.
I hide you in a cloud, that none may harm.
The mules stand ready at the gate. Forth, forth!
'Tis time ye had them harnessed to the hearse.

Chorus
          God grant that such a Saviour may appear,
          Who, by the power of His death may quell
          A greater Foe than all the Philistines.
          With this pure wish, we bring the dead man home
          To rest beside his fathers' dust in peace.
                    (*exeunt omnes*)

Part Two

DESCRIPTIVE CATALOGUE

ABBREVIATIONS

*   Item not located for examination

Expl. *explicit*

Inc.   *incipit*

Mi   microfilm

Ph   photostat

PL   an analogue of *Paradise Lost,* as listed in the "Descriptive Catalogue" of my *Celestial Cycle*

SA   an analogue of *Samson Agonistes*

DESCRIPTIVE CATALOGUE

Analogues are listed hereunder in chronological order. In each case where a microfilm or a photostat has been secured for the purpose of more careful study, the source of the photographic material has been noted. *Incipits* and *explicits* have been omitted in a few cases, especially in fragments of larger works and in translations.

The names of the chief characters assume many forms, not least because the Massoretic Hebrew forms differ both from the Septuagint and from the Vulgate, and mediaeval and Renaissance scholars chose variously from these sources. Thus the Hebrew form of the hero's name is *Shimshon* or (with the point over the left horn of the sibilant) *Simson*; the Septuagint gives *Sampson*; and the Vulgate has *Samson*. In the poems under review one finds *Simson, Simpson, Simpsom, Samson, Sampson, Sampsom, Sanson, Sanxon, Sansão, Sansone, and Samsone*. His father's name appears in the Hebrew as *Manoah*, in the Septuagint as *Manoe*, and in the Vulgate as *Manue*. Similarly we find *Delilah* or *Delila* in the Hebrew, *Dalida* in the Septuagint, and *Dalila* in the Vulgate. All of these variants appear in one or another of the poems under review. In order to maintain some semblance of uniformity, however, the common English forms *Samson, Delilah,* and *Manoah* are used in all the notes in the Descriptive Catalogue.

SA-1 (Hebrew)
Shophetim ("Book of Judges"), chaps. 13–16

Inc.   Vayyosiphu bene israel lasoth hara b'ene yehova . . .
Expl.   . . . vehu shapath eth-israel 'esrim shanah.

THE RAW MATERIALS of this "Samson saga" may have been circulating in oral form in the twelfth century B.C., when the Philistines, dislodged from Crete, descended with barbaric violence on the coasts of Israel and threatened the very existence of the infant Hebrew nation. Some details of the story, being current in the folklore of many races, may be older still. As analysed by William F. Albright, in his *From Stone Age to Christianity: Monotheism and the Historical Process* (Baltimore, 1940), it was probably committed to writing in the tenth century B.C., while in the Deuteronomic recension of the seventh century it was woven in with other stories to make the Book of Judges and rigorously edited towards religious edification by the addition of most of Judges 13 and minor interpolations in Judges 14, 15, and 16. Thus a rambunctious tribal hero emerges as a devoted Nazarite, consecrated from his mother's womb to a redemption of his people, even as that people's captivity to the Philistines has been ordained by Jehovah because the Israelites had gone "a-whoring after other gods."

Even so, it is difficult to see how such a character, with his wenching and his brawlings, could in due time be ranked by Christians as one of the saints of the Old Testament. The clue is to be found in the Epistle to the Hebrews, whose author, in chapter 11, after a long roll-call of those who have been victorious through faith, brings his roster to the following conclusion: "And what shall I more say? for the time would fail me to tell of Gedeon, and of Barak, and of Samson, and of Jephthae; of David also, and Samuel, and of the prophets: Who through faith subdued kingdoms, wrought righteousness, obtained promises, stopped the mouths of lions, Quenched the violence of fire, escaped the edge of the sword, out of weakness were made strong, waxed valiant in fight, turned to flight the armies of aliens."[1] In Christian, as distinct from Jewish traditions, Samson thus came to be regarded, on the alleged authority of Saint Paul, not merely as an elect believer of ancient times but, in due course, as one of the *sancti.*[2]

---

[1]Hebrews 11 : 32–34 (King James Version).
[2]Discussed in full and magistral fashion by Krouse, *Milton's Samson and the Christian Tradition* (Princeton, 1949), pp. 29–30, 108–118.

SA-2 (Greek)

JOSEPHUS, FLAVIUS. *Ioudaikê Archaiologia.* A.D. 93

Inc.   Meta de touton Palaistinoi teleutêsanta kratousi tôn
Israelitôn . . .

Expl.   Hoi de suggeneis aramenoi to sôma autou thaptousin en
Sarasa têi patridi meta tôn suggenôn.

THE JEWISH HISTORIAN, Flavius Josephus (A.D. 37–95), has
left us in chapter 8, Book v, of his *Jewish Antiquities* a
version of the Samson story that differs profoundly from
that of the Old Testament. He is known to have made use
of the Hebrew original, the Septuagint, an Aramaic translation, and the Targum, but he has written with the greatest
freedom, with abridgments, expansions, and embellishments
that are all his own. Even the names often differ. Thus
Samson's father, who is *Manoah* in the Hebrew and *Manoe*
in the Septuagint, is *Manoches* and *Manochos* in Josephus.
The woman who betrays him is *Delilah* in Hebrew, *Dalida*
and *Daleida* in the Septuagint, but *Dalala* in Josephus. His
prose style, moreover, as compared with the Septuagint and
still more with the Hebrew, is basically hypotactic. For
example, nearly all of the numerous *oratio recta* speeches in
these versions are turned by Josephus into *oratio obliqua*.

The substance of the story is changed even more, demons-
trably to glorify the Jews or to ennoble his *dramatis personae.*
He omits the Deuteronomic moral that Jehovah had brought
on the Philistine captivity because of Hebrew sinfulness.
Manoah is "among the most notable of the Danites." He has
a wife "remarkable for her beauty" and hence is fiercely
jealous of the visiting angel, even though the latter is an
apparition (*phantasma*). His final verdict on Samson is lauda-
tory: "We ought to admire his courage, his strength, and the
great-spirited nature of his death, and likewise his enduring
anger against his enemies to the very end. As for his being
ensnared by a woman, we ought to impute this to human

nature, which is liable to sin; but we must pay tribute to his pre-eminent excellence in all else."

Josephus had little influence on Christian thinking prior to the work of Petrus Comestor in the twelfth century A.D. In the sixteenth and seventeenth centuries, his vogue was prodigious. Thomas Lodge's English translation went through eight editions between 1602 and 1640. The chief effect of this extrabiblical retelling of the Samson story in the most attractive form that a patriotic Jew could devise was to enhance and ennoble a somewhat uncouth character and make him more acceptable to Christianity. In conjunction with the Epistle to the Hebrews and the patristic, scholastic, and Renaissance commentators, Josephus shared in turning Samson into a historical personage of indubitable sanctity. Josephus wrote only in terms of a prettified literalism, but the theologians did the rest.

SA-3 (Latin)

ABELARD, PETER. *Planctus Israel super Samson.* Accessible in Migne, *Patrologia Latina*, clxxviii, 1820 *et seq. Ca.* 1120

Inc.   Abyssus vere multa
               Judicia, Deus, tua,
               Eo plus formidanda,
               Quo magis sunt occulta . . .
Expl.   Nisi malis ad exitium
                    Properare certissimum
                         Cum praedictis.

THESE RHYMED LATIN VERSES by Peter Abelard (1079–1142) are largely given over to a denunciation of women in general, and of Delilah in particular, for their malign influence on mankind.

SA-4 (Greek)

PRODROMUS, THEODORUS. *Epigrammata* ("in quibus omnia utriusque Testamenti capita felicissime comprehendantur"). Accessible in Migne, *Patrologia Graeca*, cxiii, 1142–46

Inc. Tiktei Manôe, thauma, pros gêras meson,
        Kai tauta Sampsôn allo thauma, ton megan . . .
Expl. Seise d' helôn, pro d' hapas khamadis pesen apletos
        oikos,
        Sun de t' ar' allophulois hauton katepephne phonêa.

OF THE HUNDREDS OF EPIGRAMS by Theodorus, twenty-two deal with various phases of the Samson story and seven of these with Delilah. She is denounced in the most violent language. Women are more dangerous than bears, wolves, dragons, and scorpions. It is better to fall into whirlpools of fire or the sea than into the abominable baseness of women.

SA-5 (Latin)

COMESTOR, PETRUS. *Historia scholastica*. Accessible in Migne, *Patrologia Latina*, cxc, 1285–90

Inc. Rursus filii Israel peccaverunt coram Domino, et tradidit eos in manus Philistinorum quadraginta annis (Judges 13) . . .
Expl. . . . Ebrium dicit non vino, sed amore, vel satiatum, aliter legem Nazaraeorum excessisset ante tonsuram, et recessisset ab eo Dominus.

THIS NARRATIVE by Petrus Comestor (died 1179) is very close to the text of the Vulgate but he adds notes and comments of his own. A sample is his denunciation of women: "Almost every woman is greedy by nature, and inconstant, and to this I might add: What is more inconstant than water? Flame. And what more than flame? Rumour. What more than rumour? Woman. What more than woman? Nothing." Another note, apparently from the Targums, runs thus: "The Hebrews however say that the Philistines forced him to sleep with sturdy women, so that they might conceive sturdy children by him."

SA-6 (Latin)

ANONYMOUS. *The Lament of Samson*. From a Stuttgart manuscript of the thirteenth century, selection No. 283 in *The Oxford Book of Medieval Latin Verse*

Inc.   Samson, dux fortissime,
               victor Potentissime . . .
Expl.   Pro tali victoria
               Samson sit in gloria.

IN THIS POEM of 153 rhyming lines, Samson, having been invoked in prison by an unidentified interlocutor, tells the story of his early exploits and ultimate betrayal, including a verbatim quotation from the importunities of Delilah. In the last seventeen lines, he goes on to describe his final triumph and death in the temple of Dagon.

SA-7 (Middle English)

ANONYMOUS. *Cursor Mundi. Ca.* A.D. 1320. Ed. Richard Morris, London: Early English Text Society, 1875

Inc.   Efter him, this ilk labdon,
               Thair dempster was sir sampson
               That was so bald and wight and strang . . .
Expl.   That hus he feld, gaf naman grith,
               And slogh his faas, him-self thar with.

WRITTEN IN NORTHUMBRIA, this colossal poem of some 30,000 lines survives in several fourteenth-century versions. The Samson extract quoted above consists of lines 7,083–7,262 in MS Cotton Vesp. A.iii, British Museum. Three other manuscripts, all with textual differences, are in the Bodleian Library, the library of Trinity College (Cambridge) and the library of Göttingen University. Some critics regard it as a narrative parallel to the great corpus of the dramatic mysteries. It varies at some points in its treatment of Samson. Thus Delilah, after Samson's blinding, marries one of the Philistines, and it is at her wedding that the Hebrew hero pulls down the building. The episode begins:

> A man son o that ilk nacion
> Gun dalidam hijs wijf at wedd;
> Sampson was to the bridal ledd . . .

SA-8 (Old French)

MACÉ DE LA CHARITÉ. *La Bible et le Nouveau Testament Moralisez et mis en Vers.* A.D. 1343. Mi: University of Notre Dame (Mediaeval Institute), courtesy of Father Beichner

Inc.   Li filistins qui Dieu ne creant
          Et les ydoles doratins . . .
Expl.   Apres la mort [de] Sanson fortin
          Prent li lines des iuges fin.

THIS ALMOST INTERMINABLE POEM in rhymed octosyllabic couplets covers most of the range of Holy Scripture. Its author's version of the story of Samson and Delilah pays tribute to its popularity, for at one point he asks rhetorical questions: What poet does not know this tale? What mystery play has not presented it?

SA-9 (Italian)

BOCCACCIO, GIOVANNI. *De casibus virorum illustrium.*
Ca. 1350. Mi: University of Toronto (edition of 1544)

Inc.   Praenunciante per angelum Deo ex Manue Israhelita quo-
         dam, et pulcherrima eius uxore, Sanson progenitus est . . .
Expl. . . . orbatusque vitam non ferens, mortem sibi constituit
         et hostibus.

THIS CHAPTER 17 of Book I of Boccaccio's lengthy work in
Latin prose was based by him on Judges, Josephus, Philo,
Augustine, and others. It proved to be immensely popular.
The chapter immediately following is entitled "In mulieres"
and is a long and bitter indictment of women: "Blandum et
exitiale malum mulier. . . ." Since Delilah is subjected to
special denunciation, it is evident that the harsh remarks of
Milton's chorus regarding women are part of an ancient
tradition in Samson literature.

SA-10 (Middle English)

CHAUCER, GEOFFREY. "The Monkes Tale," Part III
("Sampson"). *Ca.* 1375

Inc.   Loo Sampsoun, which that was annunciat
         By th' angel, longe er his nativitee . . .
Expl. That no men telle hir conseil til hir wyves
         Of swich thyng as they wolde han secree fayn,
         If that it touche hir lymes or hir lyves.

SUBTITLED by Chaucer "the Monkes Tale De Casibus Virorum Illustrium," this verse narrative is based primarily on
Boccaccio's work of that title (SA-9 above) but the portion
dealing with Samson owes much to Judges 13–16 and perhaps a little to the *Roman de la Rose*, 16,677–88. The Deuteronomic moral is almost wholly omitted and Samson is
presented as a good man of pre-eminent strength whose lack
of prudence, in dealing with a treacherous woman, led to his
tragic downfall.

*SA-11 (Middle Low German)

A Samson fragment cited by Gerlach (*Der Simsonstoff im deutschen Drama* [Berlin, 1929], pp. 8–10) as printed in *Jahrbuch des Vereins für Niederdeutsche Sprachforschung,* vi, 1880, pp. 137 *et seq. Ca.* 1400

THIS OLDEST SURVIVING DRAMATIC SPECIMEN is a sixty-line fragment of a Middle Low German play on Samson. It is suggested that this may have formed part of a long mystery play or play cycle on the Old Testament. In the manuscript item are found only the Timnath betrothal and the bridegroom's riddle—the only parts omitted in SA-13 below.

SA-12 (Middle English)

LYDGATE, JOHN. *Fall of Princes. Ca.* 1435

Inc. Who was mor myhti or strong than Sampson?
     Non mor delyuer, the Bible berth witnesse . . .
Expl. Suffre no nyhtwerm withynne your counsail kreepe,
     Thouh Dalida compleyne, crie and weepe!

THE *Fall of Princes* was a gargantuan poem of some 36,000 lines, in essence an English verse paraphrase of Laurent de Premierfait's French version of Boccaccio's *De casibus virorum illustrium* (see SA-9 above). It was written between 1430 and 1438 in the monastery of Bury St. Edmunds. In the portion dealing with Samson (I, 6,336–6,510), twenty-five stanzas in rhyme royal concentrate on the treachery of Samson's "wife" as one of the great domestic scandals of all time. If a man's own wife cannot be trusted, where shall he look for loyalty on earth? Or, as Lydgate puts it,

> For yiff wyves be founden variable,
> Wher shal husbondis fynden other stable?

SA-13 (French)

ANONYMOUS. "Comme Sanxon le fortin combat le lyon; du murmure des Philistines contre Sanxon; comme Sanxon tua mille hommes de la machoere d'une asne; comme Sanxon emporte les portes de la cite de Gaze; comme Dalida promect aux Egiptiens de sçavoir ou est la force de Sanxon; comme on coupe les cheveux a Sanxon; comme Sanxon abat une maison." Lines 27,114–28,165 of *Le Mistére du Viel Testament*, ed. Baron James de Rothschild, IV, Paris, 1882. Origin *ca.* A.D. 1450. Mi: Cornell University

Inc.   SANXON
        Sur les champs je me voys esbatre
        Pour ennuy fouyr et abatre,
        Car je suis fort merencolique . . .
Expl.   LE PREMIER
        Nous sommes departys d'icy
        A bonne heure; nous fussons mors
        Si ne fussions saillis dehors.
      Ilz trebuchent tous en la maison et meurent.

THIS IS neither a systematic following of the scriptural story nor an organized dramatic action. The play opens with Samson's fight with the lion. The whole episode of the bride at Timnath, with the riddle and its sequel, is omitted. The Philistines suddenly appear on the scene, raging with unexplained anger against Samson. The rest of the original story is followed, but the absence of motivation at the outset is naïve and disconcerting.

SA-14 (Spanish)

ANONYMOUS. *Auto de Sanson. Ca.* A.D. 1500. Mi:
Biblioteca Nacional, Madrid

THIS BRIEF RELIGIOUS PLAY, surviving only in manuscript, is written in five-line stanzas rhyming *abbab*. The characters

listed are Samson, Delilah, a wagoner, a peasant, leaders of
the people, and Philistines. Its nearest cousins in type would
be the York or the Coventry mysteries, in which, however,
no *Samson* play survives.

*SA-15 (Latin)

Lost Samson play, performed at Solothurn, Switzerland, in
1543. Listed in P. Meintel, *Schweizer Brunnen* (1931)

*SA-16 (Latin)

Lost Samson play, performed at Bern, Switzerland, in 1544.
Listed in Meintel, *Schweizer Brunnen*

SA-17 (Latin)

ZIEGLERUS, HIERONYMUS. *Samson. Tragoedia nova, ad
exemplum quomodo speranda sit divina ultio et victoria
contra Turcas, Christianitatis hostes immanissimos.*
Basel, 1547. Mi: University of Chicago

Inc.   MANUE
             Respexit omnipotens Deus me sedulo,
             Auxitque dignitatem cum substantia . . .
             Ultroque vulneri gravi opponam caput,
Expl.   PUER
             Ne mihi videndi siet occasio mali:
             Fugere libet procul, patriamque deseram.

THE EARLIEST SAMSON PLAY to go beyond the artlessness of
the mysteries is a Latin school-play by Hieronymus Zieglerus
(Jerome Ziegler), a Catholic humanist who was born in
1514 at Rotenburg on the Tauber and died in 1562 at Ingol-
stadt, where he was professor of rhetoric. From 1536 to 1548
he was a teacher in Augsburg at a Gymnasium run by the

Protestant Xystus Betuleius (cf. PL-116), a scholar who seems, both by precept and by example, to have stirred him up to dramatic activity.

Ziegler's *Samson* sticks close to the biblical sources in Judges 13–16. In technique he is influenced by Plautus and Terence (whom he mentions in his Prologue) and shows no knowledge whatever of Greek drama. The play is formally divided into five acts and twenty-three scenes, and is written throughout in the iambic senarius. There is no chorus, nor are there any unities of time or place. The action extends from before Samson's marriage to the woman at Timnath down to his death at Gaza, and the settings are as various as a town of the Israelites, Timnath, the rock Etam, Delilah's bed chamber and the temple of Dagon. The two neighbours, Eleasar and Heber, who discuss the affairs of young Samson with his father, are familiar figures from Roman comedy. Ziegler has a Senecan taste for horrors, as when Samson's eyes, like Gloucester's, are put out on the stage or when the boy who announces the wrecking of the temple dwells on the carnage that resulted.

As a schoolmaster writing a play for schoolboys, Ziegler does not focus his theme on issues of theology, politics, or the psychology of sex. His conclusion is that Samson's fate comes upon him because he has been unfaithful to the morals and customs of his fathers. Again and again he returns to Philistine women, against the good counsel of his countrymen, and at last pays the penalty. The resolution of forces comes in Samson's realization of his offence and in his expiation of it. There is also the moral that women must not be given the mastery. The more questionable aspects of Samson's relations with Delilah are quietly slurred over. There is no hint of Samson prefiguring Christ.

The characters are stilted and lacking in life and the dramaturgy is that of a groping amateur. Ziegler's Latin style also leaves much to be desired.

*SA-18 (Latin)

Lost Samson play, performed at Zurich, Switzerland, in 1550. Listed in Meintel, *Schweizer Brunnen*

*SA-19 (Latin)

Lost Samson play, performed at Freiburg, Switzerland, in 1551. Listed in Meintel, *Schweizer Brunnen*

*SA-20 (Italian)

ROSELLI, ALESSANDRO. *La Rappresentatione di Sansone.* Florence, 1551. Mi: British Museum

Inc.   ANGELUS

> Silentio udite l'omnipotente Dio
> per liberare il popol d'Israelle
> del sangue Filisteo crudel e rio . . .

Expl.   SANSONE

> La voce mia signor accetta et prendi
> o Dio di Abram miserere mei
> muoia Sanson con tutti e Filistei.
> (El palazzo cade et sassi un monte d'huomini.)

EVEN MORE PRIMITIVE than Ziegler's *Samson* is an Italian play by Alessandro Roselli, written in *ottava rima*. An angel prologuizes and expounds the argument.

The action consists of a series of brief, naïvely presented episodes, covering most of the scriptural narrative. Thus Samson goes to Timnath and at once hails his bride-to-be with abrupt finality. He then immediately returns home and asks his father to arrange for the marriage. At a later stage, the flattery of Delilah is short but fulsome:

> Ah, my sweet darling, my dear one,
> Why do you cause me these pangs
> So as to beguile me with love? . . .

The play ends with Samson's petition to God for strength and the simple statement that the palace is falling.

There is no symbolism in Roselli's play. Its obvious purpose is moral, and this is most clearly worked out in the earlier scenes where Israel is represented as suffering because of apostasy. Manoah and the other Jews express their penitence, and at the urging of Samson they all sacrifice and sing a Latin hymn of supplication to God. In his heroic end, Samson is the instrument of God's power against their enemies.

SA-21 (German)

SACHS, HANS. *Tragedia der richter Simson*, 1556.
Ph: Harvard University

Inc.   HERALD
Heil und gnadt sey den ehrnvesten,
Erbern und ausserwelten gesten,
So hie entgegn versamelt sein! . . .

Expl.   HERALD
Christus, der himelisch Simson,
Erlöset gnedig iedermon . . .
Da ewig freudt uns aufferwachs.
Darzu helf uns Got, wünscht H. Sachs.

THE PROLIFIC FOLK-DRAMATIST, Hans Sachs, turned out a five-act tragedy on this theme, dated January 11, 1556. Most of the play is little more than a rhyming paraphrase of Judges 13–16, taken almost literally from Luther's translation. A herald recapitulates the argument at the very beginning, and appears again at the end of the play to comment on the significance of the action:

Samson is an emblem of Christ,
Whose incarnation and birth
Were also foretold by an angel,
And also that he should redeem his people
From their sins and from all evil . . .

In spite of this deliberate didactic purpose on Sach's part, his zestful interest in Delilah rather upsets the balance of the play. She becomes a dynamic character, conscious of her sexual power, and tends to steal the show. The only hint of classical drama is the use of a boy to announce Samson's death at the close.

SA-22 (German)

ROTBLETZ, MATTHEUS. *Samson. Die histori wie der starck Samson von synem wyb unnd nachmalen durch die Mätsen Delila betrogen und ymb syn stercke kommen ist.*
Bern, 1558. Ph: University of Chicago

Inc.	ERST NARR.
	Djewyl es darzu kommen ist
	Das d Narren wend syn zvorderist
	In allen spilen und ouch sachen . . .
Expl.	Also hand wirs Spil bracht zum end;
	Gott uns allen syn friden send.

ONE OF THE LONGEST of all the Samson plays is that published in 1558 by Mattheus Rotbletz, a Swiss schoolmaster of the Reformed Church group. Rotbletz was born in 1525, the son of a Swiss pastor; he received a humanistic education at Basel; he was thrice married, had a very large family, and died in poverty in 1578. His *Samson* was played in Aarau on August 15, 1557, with some sixty characters taking part.

He gives the Book of Judges as his source and lays an open claim to originality:

> Although the story is a very old one,
> It has never before been played anywhere
> In such a fashion as this.

This boast cannot be taken very literally. The theme had already been written on, played, and published by Ziegler and Sachs, and the version of Rotbletz is actually based very closely on the Latin play by Ziegler, whom he does not mention.

On the other hand, in paraphrasing and expanding Ziegler's 1,423 lines to his own 3,700, he has added many novelties of his own and has given much greater verisimilitude to his presentation, involving something of the rude but lusty vigour of sixteenth-century Swiss folk-drama.

Thus he enlivens his long play with a number of "interludes," put on by a couple of clowns or peasants, Cuny Pflugysen and Durss Gärstenwellen, represented as Philistines and talking broadly in the Bernese dialect. These interludes serve as a sort of chorus to the play, although they are closer to the porter in *Macbeth* than to the chorus of classical tragedy. In like manner he gives comic names to messengers, servants, and other minor characters, and builds up the comedy of the scenes in which they occur, with much eating and drinking and boasting and pushing about.

Still other characters are of the earth earthy, and even Delilah becomes a more credible prostitute. In Ziegler's *Samson*, the first Philistine prince merely says:

And now I shall pay out the money to Delilah;
As she has fulfilled her bargain, I consider it right.

In Rotbletz, on the contrary, a racy character called Tony Hellriegel der Bub insists on placing in her hand 130 pieces of silver from each nobleman; whereupon she invites him to spend the night with her and promises to share the wages of sin with him.

Rotbletz shows a greater awareness of the character of a popular audience by leading off in the very beginning with "the erste Narr," whose impertinences catch the interest of the crowd, and then following with "der erste Herold," who provides the Prologue proper. In the original open-air performance there even seems to have been a temple of laths pulled down in a public square by the hero. On the other hand, Rotbletz follows the dramatic catastrophe with a prolix season of moralising, presenting (*a*) Samson's misfortunes as a penalty for forsaking the *mores* of his ancestors; (*b*) a catalogue of moral and immoral women from Scripture; (c) an explanation that Samson's final destruction of his foes through his own death is a prefiguration of Christ's work on the cross.

SA-23 (Latin)

MAJOR, JOANNES. *Simson. Ca.* 1560. Available in *Delitiae Poetarum Germanorum*, ed. Janus Gruterus, Frankfurt 1612, Part iv. Mi: London Library

Inc.   Arma virumque cano Syriae qui primus in oris
     Mille viros letho maxillae misit ab ictu . . .

Expl. Christe veni: iam tempus adest, te moesta tuorum
     Vota vocant, ne necte moram, mora tristis amanti,
     Sat veniae indultum spirantibus arma Tyrannis
     Qui tibi, quique tuis gaudent illudere regnis,
     Si qua tuae nunc gentis habet te cura venito.

A POET of the period whose political motivation is strongly Protestant is Joannes Major (cf. PL-127), whose Latin epic *Simson*, written in heroic hexameters, belongs near the middle of the sixteenth century but apparently survives only in a large seventeenth-century collection of Renaissance Latin poets.

The entire poem consists of only two books, the first telling the biblical story of Samson and the second expounding its religious and political significance. The verbal borrowings from Vergil are obvious and numerous.

The exposition of the second Book elaborates with unwearied zeal the respects in which the life of Samson prefigures that of Christ, but Joannes Major is much more exercised over its application to the lot of the Protestants in sixteenth-century Europe. To him the Pope and the Turk are the twin pillars of the temple of Dagon, while the Protestants are the chosen people of God; and the poem ends with an appeal to Christ, the celestial Samson, to come and take the part of his people.

SA-24 (English)

ANONYMOUS. *A most excellent and Famous Ditty of Sampson, Judge of Israel. To the tune of the Spanish pavin.* London, 1563–64. Mi: British Museum

Inc.　　When Sampson was a tall young man
　　　　His power and strength increased than
　　　　And in the host and Tribe of Dan
　　　　　　The Lord did blesse him still . . .

Expl.　　So that with griefe and deadly paine
　　　　Three thousand persons there was slaine.
　　　　Thus Sampson there with all his traine,
　　　　　　Was brainèd.

THIS IS A DOGGEREL NARRATIVE, designed for singing to a Spanish dance-tune. It covers most of the Samson story.

SA-25 (Latin)

FABRICIUS, ANDREAS. *Samson. Tragoedia nova.* Cologne, 1569. Mi: Stiftsbibliothek, Klosterneuburg, bei Wien

Inc.　　GAVAL
　　　　O rector et dux temporum, qui ortu tuo
　　　　Orbem serenas, resque cunctas excitas . . .

Expl.　　　　Nutat domus toto. Hoi viri,
　　　　Hoi, perimus. Hoi . . .

A CONSIDERABLE ARTISTIC ADVANCE on any earlier version is to be found in a Latin play by Andreas Fabricius, staged at Munich in February 1568 to honour the wedding of the heir to the Bavarian throne. The author was a Jesuit, a man of wide culture and political experience, and an ardent agent of the Counter-Reformation. The Prologue recapitulates the argument and pays tribute to the religious zeal of the *Principes Bavariae.* The *dramatis personae* are as numerous as in Ziegler and Rotbletz, for Fabricius has twenty named characters in addition to a chorus, a crowd of Philistines, and Philistine soldiers. Among the former are such Terentian types as *Nochel leno* (a pimp) and *Sobaea famula Dalilae* (Sobaea, Delilah's nurse). Delilah is frankly listed as a whore (*meretrix*).

There is a marked structural advance in beginning the play directly with chapter 15 of the Book of Judges, and suspense is built up by delaying the appearance of Samson until the fifth and last scene of Act I, after other characters have been talking about him with increasing excitement during the first four scenes. Scene 1 opens with Gaval, Samson's father-in-law, lamenting the trouble that his new son-in-law has brought him with his expense and his riddle. He then tells how Samson, incensed by the dishonest ferreting out of his secret, has gone off home, and the bride has been given to another. Scene 2 reports the killing of thirty Philistines for the sake of their garments. In Scene 3, after the reported episode of the foxes, the Philistines come and destroy the bride and her parents. Scene 4 presents the increasing alarm and fury of the Philistines. Only then does the powerful source of all this upheaval appear on the stage and announce, in soliloquy, that he has resolved on still greater revenge.

Act II presents the exploit with the ass's jawbone, Act III Delilah's unsuccessful temptations, Act IV the betrayal, and Act V the final vengeance. The action ends with shrieks from the Philistines and an eloquently broken half-line.

Fabricius used his play for political purposes, and especially as a warning against marriage with heretics. In his Prologue he stresses more than physical unchastity the spiritual unchastity of relations with heretics and heretical teaching. The Bavarian duke, Albrecht, is cited as a second Samson, a mighty champion of the Catholic faith. In his choruses and Epilogue Fabricius also suggests, like Ziegler, that the Philistines may typify the Turks. The prefiguration theme is also included and the warning to hot-blooded youth against women. A blending of national and religious purpose may be found in Samson's last appeal to God:

> Arise, O God, and vindicate thy cause!
> Arise at last! I ask for nothing for myself.
> The cause is thine, thy honour is here violated . . .

Fabricius shows his familiarity with classical drama by using a variety of metres for his choruses and by varying the patterns of his choruses and semi-choruses. While his Latinity is vastly superior to that of Ziegler, he remains, however, more of a rhetorician than a poet. He is especially given to plays on words, as when Samson says of Delilah "Quanta est ocellis, bella quam labella sunt" or the Pimp says of Samson "Astutus astutam fefellit Delilam."

There is little evidence of any influence from earlier versions. Delilah's last exit, when she invites the Pimp to carry her ill-gotten money, is reminiscent of Rotbletz, but the resemblance may be only a coincidence.

SA-26 (Latin)

WUNSTIUS, MARCUS ANDREAS. *Simson, Tragoedia Sacra.* Strassburg, before 1600. Ph: Göttingen, edition of 1604. For English translation, see above, pp. 12–59

Inc.   ELUMA
> Tardum relictis effero tectis pedem
> Incurva baculo membra sustentans anus . . .

Expl.   ELUMA
> Nec statuet alius luctui finem dies,
> Quam corpori qui spiritum demet meo.

NEXT TO MILTON HIMSELF, the poet who has treated the Samson theme with the greatest freedom and the greatest awareness of classical precedent is Marcus Andreas Wunstius, a Protestant schoolman of Strassburg, who died in 1600, leaving behind him a 1,400-line Latin verse tragedy on the subject. Four years later this play, "episodiis aliquot aucta," was performed publicly by the First Class in the Gymnasium at Strassburg and the augmented version was printed forthwith. Fortunately, these additional episodes, which add 1,100 lines to the play, are printed in italics, and we are therefore able to isolate the original drama as written by Wunstius himself. The episodes are of no special interest, for they crowd the stage with miscellaneous characters and insist on rehearsing the whole action, from the Timnath bride down, in a noisy style reminiscent of Rotbletz.

The *Ur-Simson* of Wunstius is indebted to Greek rather than to Latin drama. Apart from the chorus of Hebrew maidens and some mutes, he never has more than two characters on the stage at one time. On the whole, his handling of the chorus is more like Sophocles than like Euripides; although the relation between Samson's mother and the chorus is obviously modelled after the *Hecuba* of Euripides. The main characters, apart from a herald, a barber, and a boy, are Samson, Eluma his aged mother, a priest, Delilah, and a Philistine prince. Samson and his mother are essentially dynamic characters, whose personalities evolve in the course of the action; the others are static. Wunstius is original in making Samson's mother the main figure in the foreground, dominating acts I and V. She is the dramatic "antagonist" of her son and interprets the divine will to him.

There are three dramatic climaxes in the play: (i) when Eluma warns her arrogant son against the course of the world but he leaves her in a spirit of *hybris* to enter Gaza; (ii) the deception by Delilah (Act III), through which his *hybris* is brought low; and (iii) the emotional culminating point in the mother's experience (Act V) as the dynamic of emotion prevails for a time over the static of reflexion.

There is a dangerous tendency in Wunstius to let a skeleton of ideas show through the flesh of personality, as when the motivation tends to become a struggle between the divine and the secular principles in life. On the whole, however, Samson develops from a self-sufficient youth, rash and eager for action, into a champion of God, tried by suffering. The deeply intellectual structure of the drama was evidently beyond the appreciative powers of those who decked it out with the garish trappings of popular drama before they ventured to stage it. This is perhaps in keeping with the plaintive remark in Wunstius' own Latin Preface: "for fifteen years now I have been living exiled from communion with scholars and surrounded by rustic and utterly illiterate men."

Wunstius has marked qualities of style and the dialogue closely portrays emotion, e.g. in Eluma's threefold repetition in her farewell to her son:

> Et osculum hoc, et hoc, et hoc novissimum.

His choruses are highly lyric and he has unusual gifts of metaphor, e.g. in the tribute of the chorus to the dead Samson near the end of Act V:

> Simsone in festo pereunte fato,
> Gentis Hebraeae cedidit corona,
> Murus, arx, fulcrum, columen, columna,
>   Turris, asylum.

Eluma, in her anxiety in Act V lest her son, by his self-destruction, might have damned his soul forever, reproduces a frequent debate of the theologians. Thus Augustine, in his *De civitate Dei*, devotes one chapter to the problem of Samson's "suicide" and justifies it because he was impelled by God, while Cardinal Cajetan, in the sixteenth century, also argues on his behalf. Milton's contemporary, John Lightfoot, however, holds Samson foully guilty of *felo-de-se*.

Perhaps the most instructive by-product of a study of this play may be found in a comparison with the Samson dramas of Vondel and Milton. Critics who have examined only the latter two have been prone to dismiss their resemblances in setting and treatment as being only the inevitable result of two classically inspired writers approaching the same biblical theme from the same dramatic premises. Wunstius shows that a Renaissance dramatist who has been steeped in Attic tragedy can develop a drama that differs profoundly from either Vondel or Milton. Their "inevitable" similarity turns out not to be inevitable after all.

SA-27 (Latin)

RHODIUS, THEODORUS. *Simson.* Heidelberg *et alibi* (1600, 1602, 1607, 1615, 1616, 1619, 1625). Ph: University of Göttingen

Inc. SIMSON
> Humana tempus mutat et veniens dies,
> Et irritum etiam, quod ratum fuerat, facit . . .

Expl. CHORUS
> Huc, huc onus portate cari corporis . . .
> At dum perempto huic imus exequias Duci,
> Judaea amorem voce lamentabili
> Et lacrimis testetur ac luctu suum.

THE SAME SORT OF REVISIONARY ADULTERATION that affected Wunstius' tragedy also overtook a Samson play by another Lutheran scholar, Theodorus Rhodius. The initial version, written under Greek influence, observed the classical unities of time and place. The action was set in the street outside of Delilah's home, and all five acts dealt with the day of Samson's final temptation and blinding. Prefixed to later editions, however, was a note from the author to his readers, stating that in his dissatisfaction with his first draft he had revised it "in countless places . . . past recognition" and had also added many pages. These include a scene in the streets of Gaza on the fatal holiday and a message of death brought from the ruined temple to a male chorus of Hebrews by a boy who had been the blind Samson's guide. The play ends with a funeral march and the verdict of the chorus on their dead hero. Extra opening scenes had carried the action still farther back in time to the Timnath affair. The play thus became a series of episodes rather than an organic tragedy. An English translation of the last ninety-seven lines of the inflated edition may be found on pp. 60–65.

SA-28 (German)

ANONYMOUS. *Drey schöne weltliche Lieder von Samson der Held.* Mi: British Museum

I

Inc.	Wo ist der Philistäer Heer,
	wo sind die Kriegeschaaren?
	kommt her mit eurem Ritterspeer,
	so Dalilam bewahren . . .
Expl.	liebt vorsichtig, nicht gleich wie ich,
	sonst wirds euch auch so gehen.

II

Inc.	Wer schaft neue Kopfmatrassen,
	nach der Mode austasirt . . .
Expl.	so wird sich mein Beutel mehren,
	denn ich bin ein armer Tropf.

III

Inc.	Soll mein Schatzerl, das ich kenne,
	etwas schlechtes seyn, ach nein! . . .
Expl.	Ehreneich und Gstreng sich nennen,
	kurz, kein schlechter Lump nicht seyn.

THESE "THREE FINE SECULAR SONGS" probably date from about A.D. 1600. The first is a duet between Samson and Delilah; the other two are equally artless rhymes on the Samson theme.

*SA-29 (Italian)

SANDRINELLI, BERNARDO. *Sansone accecato da' Filistei.*
Venice, 1600

*SA-30 (Latin)

Lost Samson play, performed at Basel, Switzerland, in 1600.
Listed in Meintel, *Schweizer Brunnen*

*SA-31 (German)

SPANGENBERG, WOLFART. German translation of Wunstius
(SA-26). No longer extant

*SA-32 (Portuguese)

QUINTANILLA, VAZ. *Auto de Sansão.* Ca. 1600

*SA-33 (English)

Lost Samson play by EDWARD JUBYE and SAMUEL ROWLEY.
Ca. 1602. Listed in Halliwell, *Dictionary of Old English
Plays,* p. 219

*SA-34 (Czech)

ANONYMOUS. *Historia duchowni a Samsonowi silem.* Prague,
1608

*SA-35 (Latin)

Jesuit dialogue, MS at Paderborn. Gerlach, who cites it (*Der
Simsonstoff im Deutschen Drama,* p. 54), also records his
inability to examine it

SA-36 (French)

VILLE TOUSTAIN, SIEUR DE. *Tragédie nouvelle de Samson le fort*. Rouen, undated but *ca.* 1610. Mi: Bibliothèque Nationale, Paris

Inc.

> MANUE
>> Comme apres les éclats d'un orage effroyable
>> On void du clair Phoebus la clarté agreable . . .

Expl.

> (SOLDAT PHILISTIN)
>> Sus sus, sauvons-nous; donc ce sinistre accident
>> Me doit de leur malheur faire sage et prudent.

THIS IS A FORMAL DRAMA in heroic couplets. Ten characters are listed: Manue, Samson le Fort, le Prince des Philistins, le Heraut, le Prince de Inda, le Capitaine Philistin, le Lieutenant de la lignée de Inda, le Soldat Philistin, Le messager, Dalide Courtisane Philistine. There is no chorus. Manoah gives the introductory exposition and Samson is launched in full indignation over the treatment inflicted on his bride. There are four acts and eight scenes, with no attempt to maintain unities of any sort. Act II presents Samson's earlier revenge on the Philistines; Act III portrays his betrayal by Delilah; while Act IV ends with his overthrow of the temple of Dagon. There is a long closing speech by the sole survivor, a Philistine soldier caught half dead among the wreckage.

*SA-37 (German)

ANONYMOUS. *Samsons Stärkung durch den Honig*. Jesuit Corpus Christi play at Vienna, ref. in Bernhardt Duhr, *Geschichte der Jesuiten in den Ländern deutscher Zunge* (Berlin, 1907–13), II, Part i, p. 671

SA-38 (Dutch)

KONING, ABRAHAM DE. *Simsons Treur-spel*. Amsterdam, 1618.
Mi: University of Utrecht

Inc.

SIMSON

> Hoewel hat ick ghevoel mijn sterekt so groot en grof
> Dat ick door dese Handt verstoegh ter neer in't stof
> Een Leeuw . . .

Expl.

REY DER IOODTSCHE

> Dijn's Vaders huys beschrey die niet weer komen kan,
> Die Wt levender jonst treurer-eyndich cyndt zyn daghen.

THIS DUTCH DRAMA represents an advance on all of its predecessors except the *Simson* of Wunstius. The metre of the dialogue is the heroic couplet (Alexandrines), while there are elaborate lyric utterances by two choruses, one Philistine and the other Jewish, and Delilah sings three songs, one of them, in Act I, Scene i, confessing her love to Samson. There are no stage directions but all of the action could take place in Gaza during the last few days of Samson's life. There are very few characters: Samson, Delilah, five Philistine princes (who act as a group), a lad, an executioner, a farmer, a ghost, Hilla, and Barneus.

At the outset, Delilah is sincerely in love with Samson, but the Philistine princes keep plying her with money and appeals to patriotism until she finally wails: "Ah that I had never been born! Alas! Ah, Delilah!" In the four scenes of Act II we have the several attempts to discover the secret of Samson's strength, ending in his final betrayal: "Ach Heer, ick ben verraen!" The third and final Act presents the lamentation of Samson and the Jewish chorus and the jubilation of the princes and the Philistine chorus. The princes "are sitting high up in the temple at a banquet with Delilah." Samson, after a brief conversation with the lad Amri, pulls down the temple. The Jewish chorus ends with a Euripidean epilogue on the meaning of the tragedy. While the play is more compact than most of its predecessors, it shows little ingenuity in dramatic invention, except perhaps in presenting the ghost of the cremated Timnite. It is interesting to note the explicit reference in the opening Argument to "Samson, a prefiguring of our Lord Jesus Christ and a marvellous wonder in his time." In keeping with this theological assumption, the more unseemly aspects of Samson's life are largely suppressed.

*SA-39

Jesuit play at Emmerich. Mentioned in Duhr, *Geschichte der Jesuiten*, II, Part i, p. 674

*SA-40 (Latin)

LUMMINÄUS A MARKA, JACOB CORNELIUS. *Sampson*. Contained in *Musae lacrymantes sive Plaias tragica*. Douai, 1628

ACCORDING TO Kurt Gerlach (*Der Simsonstoff im deutschen Drama*, p. 53), this lyric drama in Latin is a dialogue of the familiar school type, consisting of only five scenes and limited to the Delilah episode.

*SA-41 (Italian)

GALATÀ, VINCENZO. *La Dalida*. Venice, 1630

SA-42 (English)

QUARLES, FRANCIS. *The Historie of Sampson*. London, 1631. Ph: Library of Congress

Inc.   Within the tents of Zorah dwelt a man
         Of *Jacobs* seed, and of the tribe of Dan,

Known by the name of Monoah; to whom
Heaven had deny'd the treasure of the womb ...

Expl.   I may discard my flesh with joy, and quit
My better part of this false earth; and it
Of some more sin, and for this transitory
And tedious life, enjoy a life of Glory.

STILL CLOSER TO MILTON in time and place is Francis Quarles's 3,468-line heroic poem, *The Historie of Sampson*, printed not far from Milton's quarters in London in 1642. This rather pedestrian epic is substantially a prolix paraphrase of the Old Testament story of Samson, divided into twenty-three sections and made still more tedious in pace by appending a long versified "meditation" to each instalment, setting forth the prevailing theological interpretations of the story.

The general invocation prefixed to the poem assumes the traditional form. Quarles, however, shows little awareness of artistic structure and proportion. Approximately one-third of the poem is devoted to Samson's birth and boyhood and the second third to the episode of the bride in Timnath. Only the last four sections out of twenty-three are used to cover his betrayal by Delilah and his death in the temple of Dagon.

Quarles's style is sometimes homely, sometimes quaint, sometimes overlaid with garish rhetoric; but he is also capable of a certain rough vigour. All of these qualities are revealed in his description of the Philistine lords summoning Samson to the feast.

In describing the humiliations heaped upon Samson, Quarles is able to imply, by the mere overtones of language, a comparison with the mockeries heaped upon the blind-folded Christ by Pilate's soldiery. Parallels with Milton are few, slight, and probably accidental. An interesting discussion of Quarles and Milton may be found in George Wesley Whiting's *Milton's Literary Milieu* (Chapel Hill, 1939), pp. 251–264, but there is significantly little reference to other early analogues or to the boundless harvest of the commentaries.

*SA-43 (Danish)

RANCH, HIERONYMUS JUSTESEN. *Samsons Faengsel.*
Aarhus, 1633

Inc.   SAMSON
            Io mier oc mier ieg grunnde maa,
            Dog kannd ieg dette ey allt forstaa,
            Att gud oss iettede Canans lannd
            Att legge unnder Israells hanndt . . .

Expl.   EPILOGUS
            Der for var dig for hendis Ijd,
            Giör Poenitentz i Naadens Tid,
            Gud giff der til sin Naade!

THE AUTHOR of this rather long five-act play, *Samson's Impris-
onment,* was a Lutheran clergyman, Hieronymus Justesen
Ranch (1539–1607), a graduate of Wittenberg University.

He begins his drama with the episode of the harlot in
Gaza (Judges 16), and develops his action with a good deal
of freedom. His characters are organized characteristically by
households. Thus, Molitor, the prison-miller who lodges
Samson, has a wife, Golde, two apprentices, "Rag i Bing"
and "Saeck om Ring," and two girls, "Tom Saeck" and
"Rundze Posse"; the senior prince of the Philistines, Ahiabel,
has two small sons, Seram and Serim; while Delilah has two
maidservants, Abdon and Sapha.

In Act II, Samson twice deceives Delilah as to the source
of his strength. In each case her two maidservants sing a song
—the one on the story of Vulcan snaring Mars in Venus' bed
and the other on Venus and Cupid—and bind him as directed.
In Act III he reveals his secret and is shorn, captured, and
blinded. Act IV deliberately delays the action by picturing
Samson toiling at the mill, where the miller sings a long
amusing song. Samson turns to God for help. As Act V
opens, the priests of Dagon rejoice and sacrifice a live cat and
a live hare to their deity. Samson is brought in and subjected
to a long ordeal of insult. He prays for strength and pulls

down the temple of Dagon. Ranch then introduces five devils who chant their joy over three thousand Philistine souls indubitably headed for Hell. An epilogue stresses the importance of always being faithful to the will of God.

The author uses rhymed verse throughout, usually in couplets but sometimes with stanzas and interwoven rhymes. His dramatic bent is towards comedy and farce, rather than towards tragedy. Most typical of his quality is the ribaldry of the miller and his mates and the glee of the devils. The psychology is superficial and his hero Samson is lacking in personality.

SA-44 (Spanish)

MONTALVÁN, JUAN PEREZ DE. "El Valiente Nazareno," being pp. 89–111 in his *Comedias*, II, Madrid, 1638. Mi: Biblioteca Nacional, Madrid

Inc.   *Tocan caxas, y trompetas, y van saliendo por su orden Nacor, Antelio, Zabulon, Soldados Filisteos, Emanuel viejo, padre de Sanson, preso, y atadas las manos. Diana Infanta de Siria, Jabin Capitan, Alfea criada, y Lisarco Rey de los Filisteos, y dizen dentro.*

>REY
>>Vivo no ha de quedar ningun Soldado.
>
>EMA
>>Sr. padre de Sanson, que culpa ha sido? . . .

Expl.   SANSON
>>Aqui morirà Sanson
>>y todos los Filisteos,
>>por amigo de Dios èl,
>>y por enemigos ellos.

THIS COURT DRAMA has been heavily infected with the qualities of the heroic romance. It is also, by the way, one of the rare instances where Delilah is presented as Samson's wife, rather than as a harlot.

While not intrinsically important, it had many descendants. It was translated into Flemish by Claude de Grieck (SA-52) and into Italian prose by Riccoboni (SA-59). This latter version was turned into French by Fréret and into German by Weiskern (SA-69). Fréret's prose was in turn made the basis for Romagnési's superlatively popular verse drama (SA-65). Montalván (1602–1638) was an ardent disciple of Lope de Vega.

SA-45 (Italian)

GIATTINI, VINCENZO. *Il Sansone: Dialogo per Musica*. Palermo, Pietro de Isola, 1638. Musica di Sig. Piero Paolo Laurenti. Ph: Rome. For English translation, see pp. 66–76

Inc.   DALIDA
            Sansone è in catena.
            Non più si paventi . . .
Expl.   CAPITANO
            Non però son qui ristrette
            Le sue glorie, ov' Egli ha pace.

IT IS RARELY MENTIONED that an oratorio on the Samson theme was published in Palermo in 1638, the very year that Milton arrived in Italy for a stay of nearly a twelvemonth. Whether *Il Sansone*, by Vincenzo Giattini, was seen, heard, or read by Milton we simply do not know. One may argue that a work so close to his interests could hardly have escaped his attention and that it was probably in the "chest or two of choice music books" that he shipped to England in 1639; but all this is pure speculation.

There are four characters in the "dialogo per musica": Delilah, a Philistine Captain, a Philistine Prince, and Samson. The action is limited to the last day of Samson's life. Delilah and the Prince mock his defeat and he in turn laments his blindness and weakness. Part I ends with Samson's certainty that God will yet have mercy on him and will punish his enemies. In Part II, in the temple of Dagon, Delilah again reviles him and his God, while the Prince and the Captain cheer her to the echo. Indignant at the scorn shown to Jehovah, Samson prays for strength and pulls down the temple. The last voice is that of the Captain, half dead amid the rubble, paying tribute to the glory and peace achieved by his enemy in the universal death.

The libretto has an elaborate pattern of feminine rhymes. There is no chorus.

A second edition, published at Forli eighty years later, on the occasion of a public performance in the hall of the state palace, added an irrelevant eleven-line epilogue in honour of the Most Holy Virgin of the Fire. In this edition, the "Dialogo per Musica" is termed an "oratorio" but the original music by Pier Paolo Laurenti is still in use.

*SA-46 (Spanish)

ROJAS Y ZORRILLA, FRANCISCO DE. A lost play, acted in Madrid in 1641 but not printed. Cf. A. F. von Schack, *Geschichte der dramatischen Literatur und Kunst in Spanien,* III (Stuttgart, 1877), Nachträge 73

SA-47 (English)

ANONYMOUS. *Sampsons Foxes agreed to fire a Kingdom, Or, The Jesuit and the Puritan, met in a Round, to put a King-dom out of Square.* Oxford, 1644. Mi: British Museum

Inc.   See, two rude waves, by storms together thrown,
       Roare at each other, fight, and then grow one . . .
Expl. We thanke you and our gratitude's as great
       As yours, when you thank God for being beat.

THIS LONG POEM in heroic couplets is an Anglican diatribe against both Puritan and Roman Catholic. It is in no strict sense an analogue at all, but is included here as a sample of the polemic literature of the time showing Milton's themes in common use.

*SA-48 (Latin)

Lost Jesuit play, performed at Klagenfurt in 1648. Cited by Gerlach (*Der Simonstoff im deutschen Drama*, p. 107)

SA-49 (Dutch)

VONDEL, JOOST VAN DEN. *Samson, of Heilige Wraeck, Treurspel*. Amsterdam, 1660

Inc.   DAGON

  Ick, die den ysren staf, van roest half opgegeten,
  Beneden zwaeie, en, in den helschen raet gezeten . . .

Expl.   REY

  Och gave Godt dat een verlosser moght
    verschijnen,
  Die grooter vyanden dan alle Filistijnen
  Verdelghde door de maght en nadruck van zijn
    doot.
  Wy brengen op dien wensch dit lijk in 's
    vaders schoot.

THIS PLAY, given above (pp. 77–142) in full in English translation, was written by Holland's greatest dramatist in his distressful old age. The dialogue follows the French style of heroic couplets, while the choruses are elaborately lyrical.

  George Edmundson, in his *Milton and Vondel* (London, 1885) analyses at great length the respects in which this play, *alone among some fifteen extant dramatic forerunners,*[3]

[3]If one omits the plotless oratorio by Giattini, which also presents only Samson's last day. Edmundson does not invoke the other plays.

is identical with *Samson Agonistes* in a number of striking particulars: (*a*) both observe the Greek unities of time, place, and action; (*b*) both confine themselves to the last day of Samson's life; (*c*) the settings are the same, viz., an open place near the court and Dagon's temple; (*d*) the blind Samson is led on stage by an attendant and left to rest in a somewhat retired spot; (*e*) the chorus comes upon Samson sitting thus; (*f*) Samson is to be washed and given new clothes before performing at the Dagonalia; (*g*) there appear to be a few possible echoes of Vondel's phraseology in Milton, but this may be accidental. The use of the chorus is strikingly similar, although in this respect Wunstius, with his chorus of Hebrew maidens, must also be compared. Two other correspondences—an opening soliloquy and the later use of a messenger to describe Samson's revenge and death—are found in several other plays as well. Edmundson proves that Milton knew Dutch and was continually and intimately in touch with Holland and its publishers. The resemblances between Milton and Vondel are so great and so numerous as to make Milton's acquaintance with the Dutch play almost indubitable.

Even assuming, however, that the blind Milton, as he composed his drama, preserved vague memories of the great tragedy published somewhat earlier[4] by his Dutch coeval,

---

[4] I have continued to accept the traditional late date for the composition of *Samson Agonistes*. The attempts of William R. Parker and Allan H. Gilbert (summed up in the *Philological Quarterly*, 1949) to place it two decades earlier have been completely demolished by Ernest Sirluck in the *Journal of English and Germanic Philology*, LX (1961), 773–781. His minute, painstaking analysis of their objections to the traditional date finds these "sometimes meaningless, sometimes groundless, sometimes trivial, sometimes inapplicable." Relevant background reading may be found in S. E. Sprott, *Milton's Art of Prosody* (Oxford, 1953); Ants Oras, "Milton's Blank Verse and the Chronology of His Major Poems" in *SAMLA Studies in Milton*, ed. J. Max Patrick (Gainesville, Fla., 1953); and F. T. Prince, *The Italian Element in Milton's Verse* (Oxford, 1945).

one finds the differences between the two plays far greater than their resemblances: (*a*) In Vondel the long prologue is spoken by the exultant devil-god Dagon, who supplies the exposition of the theme; (*b*) Samson's attendant is not a mute but a wordy and insulting guard; (*c*) Samson has a bell around his neck so that he may ring to passers-by for food and drink; (*d*) the chorus is made up of Hebrew maidens, while Milton uses a male chorus of Danites; (*e*) Manoah, Delilah, and Harapha are omitted entirely from the play; (*f*) Vondel's Samson has already been told of his revenge by his birth-angel, Fadaël, and merely waits in savage rancour for his hour; (*g*) the whole middle of the play, in which the unwitting Philistines, filled with a Renaissance passion for the drama, prepare for their own destruction, has no parallel in Milton; (*h*) the only suspense lies in the opposition of those, like the nun of Akkaron, who seek to prevent the fatal morality play; (*i*) there is no hint in Vondel of that inner struggle in Samson by which the despairing hero, through successive testings, becomes the resolute and exultant saint; and (*j*) at the close there is an artificial use of Samson's birth-angel as a *deus ex machina*.

Milton, whose classical scholarship was far more profound than that of the self-taught Vondel, not only is closer in spirit to the ancient Athenians but seems on repeated readings to be more reminiscent of them than of Vondel: the characterization of Delilah and Harapha is Euripidean;[5] the bare majesty of the treatment is Aeschylean; while Sophocles,

[5]In II Sam. 21 : 16–22 and I Chron. 20 : 4, 6, 8, Ha-Rapha (lit. "the giant") is the father of Ishbibenob, Sippai, Lahmi, Goliath, and an unnamed hexadactylous brother. John M. Steadman has pointed out in the *Journal of English and Germanic Philology*, LX (1961), 786–795, the dramatic fitness of having the father of the boastful but ineffectual Goliath speak in hollow belligerence in the scene with Samson. The episode evidently has debts to the O.T. as well as to Euripides (and to Renaissance comedy) and is wholly original in Milton's treatment of the Samson story.

especially in the *Oedipus Coloneus*, stands behind the characterization of Samson, the role of the chorus, and the riddle of human misery seen against a universe of mystery. We shall err if we lay too much stress on Vondel except as a great playwright who worked out the Samson theme in ways that, though superficially similar, were essentially different from the ways of Milton.

SA-50 (Italian)

FERRARI, BENEDETTO. *Il Sansone, Oratorio.* MS only, from *ca.* 1660. Mi: Biblioteca Estense, Modena

Inc.   Già la la fiamma ultrice
            divampata la messe il Filisteo le cerreri
            fumanti impassazia col pianto . . .
Expl.   Fascino all virtù fù sempre, fù sempre Amore.

BOTH WORDS AND MUSIC ARE FOUND in this unpublished manuscript. This is a more elaborate conception than the *Sansone* of Giattini. Thus there are six singing characters: Dalida, soprano; Testo, tenore; Sansone, basso; Capo de' filistei, basso; Ragione, contralto; and Senso, basso. The personified faculties, Reason and Sensuality, add a morality play flavour to the oratorio.

SA-51 (Latin)

HARDERUS, HENRICUS. *Epigrammatum Libri Tres.* Copenhagen, 1660. Cf. PL-242

IN BOOK I OF THIS COLLECTION, there are a number of Latin epigrams dealing with Samson, viz., No. 33, "Samson edita inter Philistaeos sitiens"; No. 34, "Ad Gazaeos, quorum portas abstulerat, Samson"; No. 35, "Ad Samsonem robore miraculoso ab hostium laqueis se expedientem"; No. 36, "Ad eundem, cum in sinu Dalilae tonderetur"; No. 37, "Ad eundem, amissis crinibus, captum"; and No. 38, "Samson moriturus." The author, Hendrik Harder (1642–1683), was a Danish scholar. These epigrams were among his juvenilia.

SA-52 (Flemish)

GRIECK, CLAUDE DE. *Samson, oft edel-moedighen Nazareen. Treurspel.* Brussels, 1670. Mi: University of Amsterdam

Inc.   KONINGK
            Wil al het volk om hals, en straffen hun te gader.
Expl. SAMSON
            Daer all' sijn vyanden, de Filistijnen bleven,
            Sy door een derelijck, en ongeluckigh lot,
            Als vyanden, maer hy gelijck als vriendt van
               Godt.

THIS IS SIMPLY A FAIRLY LITERAL TRANSLATION of "El Valiente Nazareno," by Juan Perez de Montalván (SA-44). The Flemish version was played in Brussels. As in the Spanish original, for example, Samson is "Captain General of the Hebrew Army," Delilah is "Niece of Lysarkus, King of Syria, a Philistine," and she has an aunt, Diana, "Infante, Sister of King Lysarkus," and two chambermaids, Alfea and Syrena.

SA-53 (English)

MILTON, JOHN. *Samson Agonistes.* London: John Starkey, 1671

LATER TO BE BASED on extracts from Milton's text was George Frederick Handel's oratorio, *Samson,* first performed at Covent Garden, London, on March 2, 1744. The composer himself regarded this as a greater work than his *Messiah.*

*SA-54 (German)

DEDEKIND, CONSTANTIN CHRISTIAN. *Simson.*
Dresden, 1676

WHILE THIS PLAY COULD NOT BE TRACKED DOWN, a fairly full analysis of it was found in Will Tissot's *Simson und Herkules in den Gestaltungen des Barock* ([Stadtroda, 1932], pp. 13–26), a doctoral dissertation at Greifswald. According to Tissot it represents a major recasting of Vondel, with a strongly religious bent and a definite prefiguration of Christ. It is also described in Gerlach (*Der Simsonstoff im deutschen Drama*, pp. 69–73).

*SA-55 (German)

MICHAELIS, PAUL. *Der Hebraeische Hercules, Oder Simson.*
Leipzig, 1678

THIS PLAY, in seven acts, is analysed in some detail in Tissot (*Simson und Herkules*, pp. 36–44) and listed by Gerlach (*Der Simsonstoff im deutschen Drama*, pp. 70, 107).

*SA-56

ROLLE, JOHANN HEINRICH. *Simson. Sine dato*

AN ORATORIO by the music director at Magdeburg. It is listed by Tissot (*Simson und Herkules*, p. 73) but not otherwise tracked down. The text was by "Prediger Patzke."

*SA-57

ZESEN, PH. VON *Simson, eine Helden- und Liebesgeschicht.*
Nürnberg, 1679

A NOVEL, analysed by Tissot (*Simson und Herkules*, pp. 57–70) and described as conventional.

SA-58 (Italian)

MAFFEI, SCIPIONE. *Il Sansone, Oratorio a Tre.*
Rome, 1699. Ph: Rome

Inc.   FIL.

Dunque resiste ancora
Questo feroce, o donna?

Expl.   SAN.

Che adeguare
La dolcezza di questo dolore.

IN THIS ORATORIO, the number of singers is reduced to a primitive minimum of three: Samson, Delilah, and a Philistine chieftain. In Part I, the Philistine reproaches Delilah for her failure to solve Samson's secret. Samson presently arrives and is flattered and enticed by her into self-betrayal. In Part II, she rouses a shorn Samson to his fate.

SA-59 (Italian)

RICCOBONI, LUIGI. *Sansone.* 1700. Mi: British Museum, of Paris reprint of 1742

Inc.   SANSONE

E ta colpa se dalla mia mane salvosse la preda. Quel Daino era troppo auvilito dallo strepito de cani . . .

Expl.   SANSONE

Pera la tirannia d'un Rè fellone, morano i Filistei, mora Sansone.

A PROSE DRAMA, with some originalities of plot. Samson is a peaceful hunter, but God's voice in a dream summons him to war. He rescues the Philistine girl, Tamnatea, from a furious lion, which he kills. Her betrothed, Acab, disputes whether he or Samson should have her as wife. Samson proposes a riddle. If Acab can guess it, he gets the girl. She ferrets the secret out of Samson and tells it to Acab. In Act III, Samson's father Emanuel and his slave Hazaël are imprisoned. Samson is brought in in chains. He bursts his fetters, puts the Philistines to flight with an ass's jawbone, and rescues Emanuel and Hazaël. Acts. IV and V are conventional.

Editions of this play were later published in Paris in 1717, 1725, and 1742, this last with a French translation facing the original Italian, page for page.

SA-60 (German)
WEISE, CHRISTIAN. *Simson.* Zittau, 1703. Mi:
Stadtbibliothek Zittau

Inc. EBAL
Est ist nun Zeit, dass ich gegenwärtig . . .
Expl. SIMSON
Meine Seele, stirb mit den Filistern.

THIS IS A BELATED SCHOOL DRAMA, intended for the amusement and moral edification of young people. The style is influenced somewhat by French classical drama; but the language is generally insipid and prosaic, patched with learned borrowings, courtly flourishes, and sentimental gallantries. Weise's list of *dramatis personae* is crammed full of lexical learning and crowds the stage with scores of important and unimportant people. Delilah is a shy and reserved girl, unwilling even to let herself be kissed before marriage. She undertakes the betrayal of Samson only as a patriotic act, especially after Egla, her lady's maid, urges the avenging of her son, whom Samson has slain. Samson comes to Delilah as a sort of rococo cavalier, full of flattery and compliments. Especially notable in the play are its frequent comic scenes.

SA-61 (German)
FEIND, BARTHOLD. *Der Fall des grossen Richters in Israel, Oder: Die abgekühlte Liebes-Rache der Debora.*
Hamburg, 1709. Mi: London Central Library

Inc. ELON
Brich an, brich an, gewünschter Tag,
Des Dagons Opffer zu bereiten!

Expl.   CHORUS
>   (*der gefangenen Juden, von innen*)
>   Ihr Tannen heult, die Zeder ist gefallen!
>   Die Herrligkeit von Israel ist hin!

THIS IS A BAROQUE LOVE-DRAMA, based on the erotic, and presents the intrigues and adventures of court gallantry rather than any tragedy of fallen heroism. It opens with a touch of rococo pastoral, in the shepherds and shepherdesses of a harvest festival. One may sum up the complicated erotic pattern by saying that Prince Elon is in love with and beloved by Delilah, who is loved by Samson, who is betrothed to Thimna, who is in love with and loved by Jotham, who is loved by the widow Debora. Samson is portrayed as a sympathetic and ingenuous hero who is doubly deceived and unfortunate in love. He is sinned against at the very beginning by Thimna, his bride, who on her very wedding day assures Jotham of her love and promises for his sake to wheedle the riddle's answer out of her naïve bridegroom. The deception is repeated, still more disastrously, by Delilah, who betrays him for the love of Elon. The play, designed primarily as entertainment, has also a strongly comic element, especially in the case of Hadar, the porter.

*SA-62 (German)

Anonymous comedy of Samson, performed at Hamburg in 1725. Ref. Gerlach (*Der Simsonstoff im deutschen Drama*, p. 107)

*SA-63 (German)

TELEMAN, Georg Philip. *Der sterbende Simson.* 1728
A LOST OPERA, vouched for by Tissot (*Simson und Herkules*, p. 89)

*SA-64 (German)

Bader, Carl. *Simson.* Play performed at Ettal, about 1730. Now lost. Cf. Gerlach (*Der Simsonstoff im deutschen Drama,* p. 107)

SA-65 (French)

Romagnési, Jean-Antoine. *Samson.* Paris, 1730. Mi: Library of Congress

Inc.

ARMILLA

Votre âme, en ce moment, doit être rassurée;
Dalila, nous entrons dans la forêt sacrée . . .

Expl.

SAMSON

C'en est fait, périssons pour le dieu des Hébreux,
Meurent les Philistins, et Samson avec eux.

THIS IS APPARENTLY THE MOST ARTISTIC and successful version of a Samson play that began in Spain, next appeared in the prose Italian version of Luigi Riccoboni (SA-59) and a prose French version by Fréret, and finally a German prose version by Friedrich Wilhelm Weiskern. Romagnési altered the plot at several points and rewrote it in the heroic couplets of the French classical stage. The result is a curious mixture of the sacred and the profane, the tragic and the comic. Of it a later critic states: "Quoiqu'on n'y trouve ni régularité ni vraisemblance, elle a eu de tout temps un succès prodigieux, surtout en province où on la jouait toujours à chaque carême avant la révolution."

The changes from Riccoboni are considerable. Thus it is Delilah, rather than Timnatea, whom Samson rescues from a lion, with the courtly comment:

"Le ciel, dont le faveur secondait mon courage,
A voulu conserver son plus parfait ouvrage."

A sample of the play's comedy is where Samson's father, Emanuel, is shut up in a tower: a slave opens the door to let Samson go in to rescue his father, but then shuts it to capture Samson; when Samson tears the door off its hinges and comes out, the slave offers him the key to carry off too. In another, later interlude of comedy, a jester, wearing Samson's helmet and long hair, pretends to be afraid of a chicken.

Romagnési's Delilah is a princess, related to Phanor, King of the Philistines. It is not she, but her confidante, Armilla, who reports the secret of Samson's hair to King Phanor and brings about his downfall. When Samson is seized, Delilah commits suicide by stabbing herself.

An anonymous play, *Samson, ou la destruction des Philistins, mélodrame heroi-comique, en cinq actes, en vers*, published in 1806 and listed in the catalogue of the Bibliothèque Nationale, has turned out, when secured in microfilm, to be another exact copy of this old stage favourite, as familiar to rural France in 1800 as *Uncle Tom's Cabin* to rural North America in 1900.

SA-66 (French)

VOLTAIRE, FRANÇOIS MARIE AROUET DE. *Samson, Tragédie Lyrique*. Paris, 1750. Mi: Harvard University

Inc.   DEUX CORIPHÉES
                Tribus captives,
                Qui sur ces rives
                Traînez vos fers . . .
Expl.   SAMSON
          J'ai réparé ma honte et j'expire en vainqueur.

THE BIBLIOTHÈQUE NATIONALE, in Paris, also has a version published in Amsterdam in 1745. The differences are slight.

This is by general admission one of Voltaire's weakest performances. A novel touch is the setting free by Samson of a crowd of Philistine prisoners in order to demonstrate his love for Delilah. In the final scene, Samson, promising to tell the Philistine King and all his court the secrets of Jehovah and the Hebrew people, has to be assured that all of his countrymen have been removed from the temple of Dagon and that all the priests and officers of the Philistine court are present. He then pulls down the building.

SA-67 (Spanish)

ANONYMOUS. *Relacion del Nazareno Sanson*. Valencia, 1762. Mi: British Museum. Another almost identical version, printed in Cordoba but without date, was also secured from the British Museum. It is entitled *Relacion. Vida y meurte de Sanson.* Still another version, little more than a badly garbled parody of the other two, was printed, without date, at Valencia as *Relacion burlesca y muy entretenida, trovando los valientes hechos de Sanson.*
This, also, is in the British Museum

Inc.   Duque excelso de Antioquia,
              Principe heroico de Tiro,
              jurado Rey de Samaria,
              grande Emperador de Egypto . . .
Expl.   y beulva a ser lo que he sido,
              pues con una piedad sola
              tantas venturas consigo.

THIS IS A BOMBASTIC MONOLOGUE by Samson, telling his whole life story from conception to death.

SA-68 (Spanish)

MARTIN, MANUEL JOSÉ. *Historia del valeroso Sanson.*
Cordoba. Undated. Mi: British Museum

Inc.   Hallabanse los hijos de Israel, despues de haber cogido la
         tierra de Canaam, en su Paz . . .

Expl. Gran Doctor S. Augustin, dice, que Sanson no pecó en
darse la muerte, por haberlo hecho por instinto del Espiri-
tu Santo.

AN UNINSPIRED PROSE VERSION of the Samson story, with
occasional explanatory comments.

SA-69 (German)

WEISKERN, FRIEDRICH WILHELM. *Samson, ein Trauerspiel
des Herrn Ludwig Riccoboni.* Vienna, 1764.
Mi: British Museum

Inc. SAMSON
Geh, mein treuer Hazael, siehe zu, ob die Tücher
gestellet und die Netze gespannet sind . . .
Expl. SAMSON
Sterbet, Philistäer! Und Samson sterbet mit euch.

A SOMEWHAT FREE TRANSLATION of Riccoboni (SA-59).
The opening, for instance, is quite new.

SA-70 (French)

VOISENON, L'ABBÉ DE. *Samson.* Paris, 1781.
Mi: Bibliothèque Nationale

Inc. CHORUS
Samson vient attaquer nos Dieux,
Défendons, conservons leur Temple . . .
Expl. CHORUS
O Dieu d'Israël! Dieu terrible!
Nous éprouvons ta fureur inflexible.

THIS IS A VERY BRIEF POETIC SCORE, presumably for an opera.
The entire action takes place at the door of the temple of the
Philistines. Samson comes to attack the temple, but is sus-
ceptible to the beauty of Delilah and acknowledges the power
of her gods through her eyes. With a sound of thunder, God
deserts him; he loses his strength and is easily captured. In a

prayer to God he confesses his sin, recovers his strength, and pulls down the temple.

SA-71 (French)

BONNACHON, LOUIS-HENRI. *Samson, Pantomime en trois actes.* Paris, 1816. Mi: Paris, Bibliothèque Nationale

Inc. Tous les Grands de la Couronne sont assemblés pour célébrer le mariage de Samson et de Dalila . . .

Expl. Le temple s'écroule presqu'entièrement et s'ensevelit avec Samson, Dalila et un grand nombre de Philistins.

IN THE ORIGINAL PANTOMIME PERFORMANCE in Paris, August 3, 1816, the author himself took the part of Samson. A *corps de ballet* provides much of the action.

SA-72 (German)

BLUMENHAGEN, WILHELM. *Simson. Dramatisches Heldengedicht in fünf Abtheilungen.* Hannover, 1816. Mi: Bibliotheca Regia Acad. Georgiae Aug.

Inc.   MILKA
          Da liegt sie sinnend schon die lange Stunde,
          Indess die Mutter drinnen heftig schmählt,
          Und auf die frischgepflückten Feigen wartet . . .

Expl.   DIKELA
          Was Dir entrissen hab' auch ich verloren.
          Die Erde kann es nie uns wiedergeben;
          Der Glaube weis't uns an ein and'res Leben.

THIS PROLIX DRAMA of 5,238 lines of blank verse is about three times the length of *Macbeth* but actually seems to have been put on the stage at Altona in 1811. The action ranges from Samson's withdrawal to the rock Etam down to the final destruction of the temple of Dagon. There are some novelties in the *dramatis personae*. At the outset, Delilah, a Philistine girl living with the Hebrews, is really in love with Samson, but her childhood lover, Talmai, son of the Philistine priest Abimilech, turns up and begins to reclaim her loyalty. Samson meanwhile is wooed and won by Dikela, daughter of Abimilech, and Samson tells Delilah that he and Dikela are to marry. Delilah, while remaining a well-loved concubine, is to be Dikela's servant. Stung by jealousy and goaded on by Talmai, for whom her love has revived, she cuts off Samson's hair and betrays him to his enemies. When Delilah later learns that the captive Samson has strangled Talmai bare-handed and that his own eyes have been gouged out, she dies of grief and remorse. After the destruction of Dagon's temple, Abimilech, who has survived the disaster, agrees with the Hebrew high priest, Eli, that the Philistines and the Hebrews shall thereafter live side by side in peace and amity. Dikela comforts and protects Samson's widowed mother, Peninna.

SA-73 (German)

ANONYMOUS. *Simson. Dramatische Skizze in drei Aufzügen.* Zürich, 1844. Mi: British Museum

Inc.   MANOAH
         Was sagst du, Hanna, zu dem neuen Bande, welcher Simson geknüpft hat . . .
Expl. MANOAH
         Und du, Jüngling, der du dich zum Herrn gewandt hast, du seiest mir der Sohn Simson's und mein Sohn, ein Bürger Israel's ewiglich.

A COMPARATIVELY CONVENTIONAL DRAMA IN PROSE. Hanna, Samson's mother, talks of Delilah as Samson's wife, but Manoah repudiates the term. In Act II, the Philistine priests and princes beleaguer Delilah with arguments, seeking to have her betray her husband. They at last succeed. Act III brings the feast of Dagon. Obed, the Philistine lad who led Samson about, reports his death and his own allegiance to Jehovah, and is adopted by Manoah.

SA-74 (German)

GÄRTNER, WILHELM. *Simson. Tragödie in fünf Handlungen.* Vienna, 1849. Mi: Hofbibliothek

Inc. PROLOG
Nicht Politik, beim Himmel! will ich singen,
Will für die Zeit nicht Wunderpillen dreh'n;
Mit meinem Leid' will ich, ein Jakob, ringen,
Weil's Abend wird, den Himmel mir beseh'n . . .

Expl. EIN ZWEITER
Auf seinen Schultern trägt er eine Säule.
JOAS
Sie sind es: Gideon, Jeftha, Simson!
ALLE (*betend*)
Gideon, Jaftha, Simson!

THIS UNWIELDY ARM-CHAIR DRAMA, written in prose, has some seventy named characters and unnumbered priests, priestesses, soldiers, and common folk. Action begins before the city of Eshtaol, shifts to the streets of Timnath, then to the chamber of Samson's bride Zalmuna, then to the rock of Etam, then to a stone quarry in the forest, then to a camp of the Iraelites, then to Delilah's throne room in Gaza, then to a dungeon, and finally to a public square in Gaza, near the temple of Dagon. Delilah is a fanatical monarchist and tries to win Samson to the acceptance of a sort of pagan kingship, with herself as consort, founded on strength, terror, and love. Before her great scene of seduction, she murders the harlot of Gaza with whom Samson has slept, drinks her blood from a goblet, and goes to anoint Samson's feet and head from an alabaster box of precious ointment. There are echoes of Shakespeare, as where Samson, like Julius Caesar, steadfastly refuses a crown offered him by the crowd, or where the gaoler and his assistant, like the two gravediggers in *Hamlet*, bandy wit back and forth: "As a thing for the begetting of mankind, love is needful and wholesome. Anything beyond that belongs in gaol." . . . "You are both patriarch and prophet and I drink with pride from the stream of your discourse." There are also anticipations of the Passion of Christ, as when Samson is being led to his death in the temple of Dagon and one priestess puts a purple robe on him ("Dieses Kleid umschliesse die Glieder des Königs der Juden!"), while another sets a crown of thorns on his head ("Diese umkränzte Hörnerzier ehre den Hohenpriester!").

SA-75 (English)

ANONYMOUS. *Poem from the Bible: Samson. Sine dato.*
Mi: British Museum

Inc.   Few natures in the world are so well mix'd
          Indulgence will not spoil them: we are flesh . . .
Expl.   And buried him in his father's burying place
          Twixt Eshtaol and Zorah; there he lies.

SOME THIRTY PAGES of fourth-rate blank-verse narrative plus a noisy rhymed ode of blood and fire in honour of "the great god Dagon." Probably about A.D. 1850, for it reveals the worst excesses of a degenerating Romantic Movement. Delilah, for example, is thus described:

> She came to him; with those destroying eyes,
> Night-lashed and alabaster-lidded; stars,
> Dark stars upon his face . . .

SA-76 (German)

MÜLLER, EDUARD. *Simson and Delila: Eine Tragödie in fünf Akten.* Breslau, 1853. Mi: British Museum

Inc.
    ILISA (*Frau des Oberpriesters Dagons*)
        Legst du nicht an den heil'gen priesterlichen
            Schmuck? . . .

Expl.
SAMSON
    Ich Dich. Ihr Säulen, stürzet! Sink' in Schutt und Staub,
    Du Haus des Gräuels!—Ew'ger, treuer Gott, erhör'
    Im Tode mich! Es sühne meine Schuld der Tod.

THIS FULL-LENGTH PLAY is mostly in unrhymed Alexandrines, but breaks out in rhymed songs on the slightest provocation. Delilah is the gentle teen-age daughter of the high priest of Dagon. She is about to be made a "Bride of Dagon" but is rescued from that fate by Samson and a band of his warriors. In Act IV, while Samson is in prison, Delilah comes to him and protests that she still loves him. Samson, however, stabs her to death with a dagger and his cell is wet with her blood. He is doomed to death by fire in the temple of Dagon. "Hinweg, zum Feuerofen, wo er braten soll!" cries her father. In the temple, however, a sudden supernatural gale puts out the altar fire; thunder and lightning burst overhead; and Samson suddenly tears his fetters apart and pulls down the main pillars of the temple. The whole play is sheer melo-drama.

SA-77 (German)
LOEWE, FRIEDRICH ANTON. *Der Tod Simsons.* Berlin, 1857.
Mi: British Museum

Inc. ERSTER AELTESTER (*zu Boas*)
    Noch einmal, Freund, lass jedes Ohr sich füllen
    Mit dieser grossen Kunde. Nicht seit Midian's . . .
Expl.   In Flammen verklärt, ein unsterbliches Paar,
    Schwebt Ihr, selige Geister.

THE DRAMA PROPER is in the time of Boaz, Naomi, and Ruth, but in the *Vorspiel* covered above, old men (*uralt*) recall the far-off days of Samson's deeds and death, as an inspiration for deeper devotion to Israel in their own day.

SA-78 (English)

BIEN, Rabbi HERMAN M. *Samson and Delilah; or, Dagon stoops to Sabaoth.* San Francisco, 1860. Harvard Library

Inc.	ANGEL
	Sacred hymns I'll chant to Thee,
	Thine eternal love and power . . .
Expl.	SAMSON
	With the Philistim will I die this day—
	The Idol fall!
	SAMSON AND NAMILAH
	Triumph for Sabaoth!

A BLANK VERSE DRAMA of no particular merit. Namilah, daughter of Bolon, Dagon's high priest, is in love with Samson, but is supplanted as his wife by the scheming Delilah. It is through alcohol that Delilah secures his secret. Namilah, disguised as a boy, tends Samson and wins him back to faith in God. Delilah dies, poisoned by her brother Plias. Namilah perishes with her Samson when he pulls down the temple.

SA-79 (French)

VIGNY, ALFRED DE. "La Colère de Samson" in *Les Destinées. Poèmes philosophiques.* Paris, 1864.

Inc.	Le désert est muet, la tente est solitaire.
	Quel pasteur courageux la dressa sur la terre . . .
Expl.	Et la délation du secret de nos cœurs
	Arraché dans nos bras par des baisers menteurs.

A POEM of 136 lines in rhymed Alexandrine couplets, dated April 7, 1839, but not published until after the poet's death. It pours into the story of Samson's betrayal and violent death the lava of Vigny's personal rage at the actress, Marie Dorval, by whom he had recently been betrayed. Women are denounced by Samson as creatures of incorrigible wickedness and deceit, and a postscript by Vigny calls on heaven and earth to punish their treachery.

SA-80 (Italian)

ASTE, IPPOLITO D'. *Sansone*. New York, 1873. Widener Library, Harvard University

Inc.   MANOA
        Sali, sali all' Eterno, o puro incenso
        D'ostia votiva . . .
Expl.   SANSONE
        Cadete, o mura . . . ch' esse quì sepolto . . .
        Io bramo . . . e vo' pur . . . che il mio popol viva!

IN THIS VERSION, Samson the Nazarite drinks wine and in his drunkenness reveals his secret to Delilah. Not Delilah, however, but a stool-pigeon named Melca, placed in the house by the Philistine prince, Lamech, reveals the secret that she has overheard. Delilah remains loyal to Samson throughout. The drama was played in the U.S.A. in 1873 by Signor Salvini and Company, and this in an English version that was printed along with the original Italian.

SA-81 (German)

RICHTER, KARL TH. *Samson*. 1875. Mi: Oesterr. Nationalbibliothek, Wien

Inc.   ELISSA
        O! lass mich, Amme lass! Ich muss hinaus!
        Des Hauses enge Luft erdrückt das Herz . . .
Expl.   NAHMOR
        Geschlecht geht um Geschlecht dabei verloren
        Und Noth und Tod durchfliegt im Kampf der Welt.

THIS IS a 2,800-line blank-verse play in five acts. Delilah, after the betrayal of Samson, realizes her love for him and seeks to free him. When freed, however, he heads the Hebrew warriors in further slaughter and dies of wounds. Delilah stabs herself to death beside his corpse. Her former lover, the Philistine King, Nahmor, gallantly provides for an honourable joint burial: "Lay both of them within one holy grave!"

SA-82 (French)

LEMAIRE, FERDINAND. *Samson et Dalila* (music by CAMILLE SAINT-SAËNS). Paris, 1877

Inc.   CHORUS
           Dieu d'Israël! écoute la prière
           De tes enfants t'implorant à genoux . . .
Expl.   SAMSON
           Qu'avec toi je me venge, ô Dieu!
           En les écrasant en ce lieu!
           Tous
           Ah!

THIS LIBRETTO by a cousin of the composer is organized in three acts:

Act I. A public place in Gaza. Samson strikes down the satrap Abimelech and drives the Philistine soldiers to flight. Delilah, priestess of Dagon, invites Samson to renew his former visits to her home in the Vale of Sorek.

Act II. Outside her home that spring evening, Delilah waits for Samson. When he arrives in the gloaming, she reproaches him for his coldness and sings the melting aria, "Mon cœur s'ouvre à ta voix . . ." As a challenge to his avowed love, she demands the secret of his strength. He reveals it and presently his capture follows.

Act III. After a brief scene in Gaza's prison, where Samson prays to God for forgiveness and help, we pass to the interior of Dagon's temple and the Bacchanalian rejoicing of the Philistines. Samson enters and is subjected to contumely. He overthrows the pillars and dies among the Philistines.

SA-83 (German)

SCHIFF, J. H. *Simson and Delila. Trauerspiel.* Stuttgart, 1877.
Mi: Universitäts- u. Stadtbibliothek, Köln

Inc.

SIMSON

Allvater, dessen Ruhm die Himmel melden,
Der Du in Deiner Güte jeden Morgen
Das Schöfungswerk (*sic*) erneust—ich preise Dich! . . .

Expl.

DELILA

Süss ist der Tod mit Dir!

SIMSON   Süss ist die Rache!

THIS MELODRAMA in five acts and thirty-seven scenes is
limited in topography to Zorah (Act I), Samson's birthplace,
and to Timnath (Acts II–V), assumed to be the capital of
the young Philistine Queen, Delilah. In Act I, Samson is
launched into warfare by a patriotic mother and chosen as
judge by the Israelites. In Act II, after a series of victories, he
breaks into Delilah's palace, sworn to kill her with his own
hand. Her beauty melts his heart and for her sake he cancels
plans to destroy Timnath. In Act III he marries the Queen
but a treacherous high priest of Dagon, Seba, who also loves
her, plots their destruction. Seba promises solemnly that if
Delilah will cut off Samson's hair, so as to keep him from
returning home to Jewry, the hero will be held sacred by
him. However, as soon as the Queen has obeyed, Seba brings
in soldiers to fetter and blind Samson. In Act IV, in the
dungeon, Seba offers Samson a choice between publicly
sacrificing to Dagon (with life and wife assured) and refusing
and being himself sacrificed. He chooses death. In Act V,
Delilah is to sacrifice Samson but stabs Seba to death instead.
While her faithful household guards protect the Queen from
the maddened priests and populace, Samson pulls down the
temple. She rejoices in dying with him.

SA-84 (Italian)

CARINO, A. *Nascita, vita e morte di Sansone*. Florence, 1878.
Mi: British Museum

Inc.   Canto le forze dell' Ebreo Campione,
                Sterminator del Popol Filisteo . . .
Expl.   Distrutti i Filistei tra le ruine,
                Fu glorioso di Sansone il fine.

A BRIEF NARRATIVE POEM in *ottava rima*, some 360 lines in length. It is little more than a fairly literal versification of the entire Samson story from the Book of Judges. It has also been printed anonymously as *Storia di Sansone*.

SA-85 (German)

HEYSE, PAUL. "Simson. Trauerspiel in einem Akt" in *Drei einaktige Trauerspiele and ein Lustspiel*. Berlin, 1884.
Mi: University of Nottingham

Inc.   ADRIEL
                Gebt Raum und haltet Ruhe!
                STIMMEN   Ruhe! Hört
                Den Haushofmeister!
Expl.   DER GREIS
                Den Enkeln von der Hochzeit Delila's
                Und von dem Blinden, dem sein Gott der Weg
                Zu Sieg and Rache wies.

THE ENTIRE PLAY TAKES PLACE, as in Vondel and Milton, on the last day of Samson's life and in an open place in Gaza before the palace. Delilah is to marry Joram, Prince of Gaza, and the people are invited to the wedding feast where blind Samson will dance and sing to amuse the company. He and the boy who leads him arrive early and sit under a pomegranate tree for most of the play. Here they are visited in turn by townspeople, Joram and Delilah, then Delilah alone, and finally Samson's mother, Achsa. Delilah, while alone with

Samson, overflows with sorrow and melts him to forgiveness. She promises to poison Prince Joram on his wedding night and then take Samson to his old home in Zorah. His mother, however, rouses him to sterner counsels, and when he is led in to sing at the feast he goes with his plan of destruction evidently in mind. He sends the boy out of the palace with orders to keep his mother at a safe distance.

SA-86 (German)

SCHEFFEL, JOSEF VICTOR VON. "Simson" in *Gedichte aus dem Nachlass.* 1889

Inc.　　　Zu Gaza im kühlen Museumssaal
　　　　　Die Philister schimpften and schalten . . .
Exp.　　　Da neigte sich das Museumsdach:
　　　　　Der Philisterball war zu Ende!

AMONG THE POSTHUMOUS POEMS published in 1889 by Scheffel's son is this lusty drinking song, telling Samson's story with great gusto in six seven-line stanzas.

SA-87 (German)

DULK, ALBERT BENNO. *Simson: Ein Bühnenstück in fünf Handlungen* (1859) in *Sämmtliche Dramen.* Stuttgart, 1893.
Mi: British Museum

Inc.
ACHSA
　　　Lass, Herrin, ruhen die geschäft'ge Hand!
　　　Schon steigt die Sonne in des Himmels Gipfel . . .
Expl.
SIMSON
　　　Du kannst nicht treffen . . . ob Du Dagon wärst!
　　　Denn sieh', hier ist der Herr and spricht: Nicht Einer
　　　Geht lebend von mir! Wehe Euch! Dies ist
　　　Die Rache Simsons and Delilahs!
DELILAH (*sich aufrichtend*)　　　　　　Amen!

SOMEWHAT IN THE INFLATED COURTLY TRADITION of Perez de Montalván and Romagnési, this version has Samson finally win Delilah's heart by his magnanimity of character. She has been a priestess of Astaroth and is the daughter of Seboa, high priest of Dagon, but in the last scene she expresses her adoration of Jehovah and her allegiance to Samson. As Prince Selai thrusts her through with a spear, she cries out to Samson to look to the temple's great central pillars. The possibility of overthrowing the building, as she suggests, appeals to him. He kneels and prays to Jehovah for strength. Prince Thohu throws a battle-axe at him but misses. Samson then tears down the temple.

SA-88 (German)

LEMMERMAYER, FRITZ. *Simson und Delila. Tragödie in fünf Akten.* Leipzig, 1893. Mi: Stadtbibliothek, Köln

Inc.
> DANIEL
>> So sitzt er Tag und Nacht und regt sich nicht.
>> Versuch' ich's neuerdings, ihn anzurufen?

Expl.
> SIMSON   Selig ist es, diese Welt
>> Des Wahnes und der Wirrnis zu verlassen! (*Stirbt.*)

THIS 2,500-line play in blank verse is scarcely viable for stage purposes. For example, the collapse of the temple occurs on stage and Samson and Delilah survive amid the dust and wreckage long enough for a ten-minute interchange of hatred and defiance, concluding in a tender farewell kiss. The most unusual character is Daga, Samson's Timnite wife, assumed to have been burned to death in the conflagration of her father's house but actually saved by an angel and living in seclusion, "nicht todt aber leblos," until Act III, when she appears in Gaza and leads Samson by the hand out of the mansion of the temptress Delilah. In Act IV, however, Delilah stabs her to death and regains control of her victim Samson. In Act V, in the temple of Dagon, Delilah crowns the blind and fettered Samson with a crown of straw and puts on him a ragged purple robe purchased from a passing beggar. All the people then mock his parody of kingship: "Heil Simson! Heil dem König!" This is, of course, in keeping with the Renaissance idea of his prefiguring Christ. Other original characters are Delilah's brother Uriel, whom Samson kills in combat before Delilah's face, and Samson's orphan sister Esther, who in Act III pleads in vain with her infatuated brother to come home.

*SA-89 (German)

ITZEROTT, MARIE. *Simson*. 1899. Cited in Gerlach (*Der Simsonstoff im deutschen Drama*, p. 84)

SA-90 (English)

SCOTT, FREDERICK GEORGE. "Samson" in *Poems Old and New*. Toronto, 1900

Inc.	Plunged in night, I sit alone Eyeless on this dungeon stone . . .
Expl.	At whose life they scorn and point, By its greatness out of joint.

IN TWENTY-TWO QUATRAINS rhyming *aabb*, Samson in his prison cell soliloquizes, then turns in a long prayer to Jehovah. He defends the excess of masculine boldness with which he revealed his secret to Delilah and begs for "one blind hour" in which his rage and power may give him a hero's end.

*SA-91 (German)

HANAU, HERMANN. *Simson*. 1902. Cited in Gerlach (*Der Simsonstoff im deutschen Drama*, p. 84)

SA-92 (German)

WETTE, HERMANN. *Simson, Tragödie in fünf Akten, nach Worten des Alten Testaments.* Leipzig, 1904. Mi: Princeton University

Inc.   SAMSON
        Der Mensch, vom Weibe geboren,
        Lebt kurze Zeit,
        Voller Unruh, Sorg and Müh.
Expl.   Die Stimme des Herrn aus der Höhe:
        Simson, stirb! du hast vollendet!
            (SIMSON *stirbt*)

THIS TWENTIETH-CENTURY PLAY is unusual in introducing, among the *dramatis personae*, "Der Herr, Drei Elohim, Satanas, der Tod, Geister und Dämonen." Delilah is a sympathetic character. In Act III, in Samson's absence, she yearns for him in the words of the Song of Solomon. The lying priest of Baal assures her that if she will cut off Samson's hair, he will not stray but will be her darling forever. In Act IV, when Samson is in prison, Satan and the demons come and torment him.

SA-93 (English)

WHIFFEN, EDWIN T. *Samson Marrying.* Boston, 1905

Inc.
    MANOAH
        With wavering hope and doubtful resolution
        Of what before so oft by me essayed,
        I have drawn thee to this place, where friendly silence...
Expl.
    CHORUS
        So foul dishonor stuck upon our front,
        This day's disgrace, our sad reproach and shame.

A TRAGEDY of some 1,400 lines of blank verse, with the choruses in irregular verse, modelled after Milton. The style is awkward and sometimes seems an open parody of Milton, as when the chorus of Philistines (p. 50) declares:

> Alas, if such thy tale, no cause of triumph
> In this appears, occasion more to wail
> And knock the breast; nothing but ill and foul . . .

This and the three following plays by the same author preserve the classical unities in each case.

SA-94 (English)

WHIFFEN, EDWIN T. *Samson at Timnah*. Boston, 1905

Inc. SAMSON
> O what a swarm of restless thoughts aroused
> Awakens in me, while I contemplate . . .

Expl. CHORUS
> As now for us, when long matured
> His high intent his purpose serves
> With vindication full and fair event.

A SIMILAR DRAMA, dealing with the slaughter made at Timnah by Samson after the Philistines had destroyed his bride and his father-in-law.

SA-95 (English)

WHIFFEN, EDWIN T. *Samson Hybristes.* Boston, 1905

Inc. PHIL. MESS.
> From utmost bound of Judah's land I come
> To Hebron old, the seat of Anakim . . .

Expl. CHORUS
> Happy, and that his high intent
> Good out of evil brings forth still;
> The event the purpose vindicates.

THE PLAY IS SET before the gates in Hebron, where the Judaean elders arraign Samson for his deeds. He is given over, bound, to the Philistines, but a messenger presently reports his slaughter of a thousand foes with the jawbone of an ass.

SA-96 (English)

WHIFFEN, EDWIN T. *Samson Blinded.* Boston, 1905

Inc.   DALILA

    Once more with doubtful hope and wavering purpose,
    Although my oft repulse contrary warn
    And promise like event, if I persist . . .

Expl. CHORUS

    His purpose high decreed, chief hope
    To us remaining, and the end
    With vindication full and fair event.

THE SCENE IS AT DELILAH'S HOUSE, in the Vale of Sorek. After considerable delay, Delilah learns the secret of her husband's strength. He is led away a blind captive to Gaza, but feels already some "rousing motions" that anticipate a triumphant outcome.

SA-97 (German)

KRUG, MARIA (Pseudonym ALINDA JACOBY). *Samson, Drama in vier Aufzügen.* Kempen (Rheinland), 1908. Mi: Köln

Inc.

    IBRAHIM   Ja,
    Das war ein Sieg! Nie sah ich seinesgleichen!

Expl.

    SAMSON

    Lass mich dem Tode die Götzendiener weih'n
    Und sterbend deiner Ehre Rächer sein!

THE FIRST TWO ACTS TAKE PLACE in and around Zorah, the last two at Gaza. Dramatic invention provides two foils to Samson: Sunim, a Philistine who is also in love with Delilah, and Jonathan, a Hebrew warrior who is jealous of Samson's exploits and so turns traitor. As a similar foil to Delilah, the

pure Hebrew maiden Rachel comes to Samson in the dungeon
and confesses her love for him. When she urges him to turn
for support to the sure mercies of God, his faith is renewed
and his old strength of body comes back. Delilah is an ambi-
valent sort of creature, wavering back and forth between her
love for Samson and the patriotism demanded by her people.
Samson forgives her in the dungeon. Elements of the supernatural are invoked in the closing stage directions: as Samson
shakes the pillars of the temple, fire breaks forth from the
ground and there is fearful lightning and thunder in the sky.

SA-98 (German)

Eulenberg, Herbert. *Simson: Eine Tragödie nebst einem
Satyrspiel.* Leipzig, 1910. Mi: Harvard University

Inc.   Daniel
         Ruht er noch immer? Wacht er nicht mehr auf? . . .
Expl. Issachar
         . . . wer jubeln kann and wer weinen muss, der soll
         Simsons gedenken unter den Menschen in Ewigkeit.

In Act i, a distraught Samson is at home with his wife Rachel
and his small sons. He is besought as a liberator by the high
priest, the Levites, and finally the whole nation. He eludes
them and disappears.

In Act II, Samson intrudes on a party in the house of Kaleb,
a rich Askelonite, and makes defiant love to his daughter
Delilah. After Samson's departure, she drinks herself tipsy
and bestows her favours on some rich loafers. "Wer will
mich," she cries, "der hat mich!"

In Act III, Samson returns home by night and tells his wife
that he no longer loves her. He sets his house on fire and
burns his wife and children to death.

In Act IV, Samson comes to Delilah's bedchamber and tells
her that he has murdered wife and children for her sake,
even as he had once killed Delilah's husband out of jealousy.

In this mood, he willingly tells her the secret of his strength
and is presently caught and blinded.

In Act V, the blind Samson pulls down the temple of
Dagon and destroys them all. The chief characteristic of this
play is that Delilah is a sex-crazy, half-naked young widow
and Samson a man infatuated to the point of madness.

SA-99 (German)

EULENBERG, HERBERT. *Satyrspiel zum Simson*. Leipzig, 1910.
Mi: Harvard University

Inc.
> MINOS
>> Hier ruht, der Simson hiess. Wir stehen hier
>> Zu richten ihn und seine ew'ge Seele . . .

Expl.
> MINOS
>> Zog sein erloschner Geist voll edler Brunst
>> Gleich diesem Purpur in den reinsten Aether.

WORTHY OF SEPARATE LISTING is this weird sequel to Eulenberg's *Simson*. The setting is before the gates of the Under-
world. The dominant character is Minos, sometime King of
Crete but now judge of the dead. Other characters are two
prosecutors ("the abstract man" and "the erudite woman"),
the body of Samson, a chorus of apes, and a voice in the
storm. The two accusers, when called on by Minos, denounce
Samson as more beast than man, and the chorus of apes
clamours to devour his body. The prosecutors cast in two
black stones as their ballots. Minos, however, throws in two
white ones; a storm arises; and a voice in the storm vindicates
Samson:

> Keiner soll sein Grabmal finden
> Von Verehrung frei und Hohn,
> Ruh' er bei den selig Blinden,
> Lorbeer um die Stirn als Lohn.

SA-100 (German)

EGGERT, EDUARD. *Simson. Tragödie in fünf Aufzügen.*
Ravensburg, 1910. Mi: University of Bonn

Inc. SIMON
　　　Wach auf, geliebte Schwester, komm ins Haus!
Expl. SIMSON
　　　Wir sind gerächt, Jehova . . . Halleluja!

THIS BLANK-VERSE PLAY is notable for its use of clairvoyance
and second sight. When Act I opens in Zorah, Zelelponi,
mother of Samson, wakens in anguish from a nightmare in
which she has seen a gleaming marble temple fall in ruins and
has found the dead body of her son beneath the wreckage.
The ultimate catastrophe is thus foreshadowed from the very
beginning. Again, in Act IV, Samson in Delilah's chamber
sees a warning spectre of his mother and talks with it, to
Delilah's dismay. In Act V, when a band of young Hebrews
seeks to rescue Samson, he has a forewarning of Jehovah's
destructive purpose for him and goes resolutely to his end, first
asking Ehud to lead him to the two central pillars of the
temple. Delilah does not betray him. An apostate Jew, Serah,
himself in love with Delilah, eavesdrops on their conversation
and hears Samson's voluntary exposure of his secret. In the
closing scene in the temple, Delilah repudiates her would-be
bridegroom, Serah, and proclaims herself to be Samson's true
wife. Serah thereupon stabs her to death and Samson pulls
down the temple.

SA-101 (German)

LEMBACH, AUGUST. *Samson. Ein Drama in vier Akten.*
Berlin, 1911. Mi: Universitätsbibliothek Berlin.

Inc. EIN VORNEHMER PHILISTER.
　　　Nun frag' ich euch, was haben diese Juden
　　　vor uns voraus, das ganz sie nach Gefallen . . .

Expl. SAMSON

>   Und lodernd mir als Todesfackel, Herr,
>   jag deiner Blitze Flammensturm zur Erde.

THIS IS a 3,200-line blank-verse play in four acts.

In Act I, the triumphant Samson meets the young virgin Delilah on the street and commands her to go with him to his camp to serve his bed. Her uncle privately tells her to use her position as Samson's wench to ferret out the secret of his strength. In Act II, after she has won and betrayed his secret, she realizes that she has come to love him. In Act III, she visits him in the mill at Gaza and woos him but is at first repulsed. At last she persuades him of her sincerity, and when her murderous uncle, Mardochai, interrupts them, they kill him and throw him down a well. Act IV is in the great hall of Gaza. The Philistines wish to slaughter Delilah, but Samson delivers her by stabbing her to death and then pulls down the pillars upon them all, just as a fearful thunderstorm breaks.

SA-102 (German)

WEDEKIND, FRANK. *Simson, oder Scham und Eifersucht. Dramatisches Gedicht in drei Akten* (1913) in *Ausgewählte Werke*, Munich, 1924. Mi: Harvard University

Inc.

CHETIM

>   Noch einmal hier?—Niemand! Vielleicht nur Simson?
>   Drei Türen. Jeden Augenblick stürzt Simson . . .

Expl.

SIMSON

>   Herr, gib mir nur dies eine Mal noch Kraft,
>   Dass ich mit einem Schlag für meine armen
>   Augen an den Philistern Rache nehme.

ACT I, set in Delilah's house, presents the betrayal and blinding of Samson. Act II shows Samson toiling in the mill. In Act III, set in the temple of Dagon, we reach the final disaster. Samson appears to be motivated more by bitter personal revenge than by any sense of a spiritual destiny.

SA-103 (German)

BURTE, HERMANN. *Simson: Ein Schauspiel.* Leipzig, 1920.

Mi: Harvard University

Inc.   PROPHET

Strahle der Sonnenschein,
Ehlicher Liebe . . .

Expl.   BUCKELCHEN

Lasst uns auf die Berge treten,
Von den Bergen kam das Licht.

THIS PLAY HAS MANY ELEMENTS OF ORIGINALITY. In Act II, Delilah, a harlot, comes to seek Samson out in the countryside and shamelessly courts him. For example, when he denounces her Philistine costume, she replies that for him she will gladly dispense with clothes:

SAM.

Du trägst die Tracht des Landes, das ich hasse.

DEL.

Willst du, so steh ich nackt vor dir!

When Philistines come and bind him, she undoes his ropes and he kills a thousand men with an ass's jawbone.

In Act III, she has a hand in his capture but opposes his blinding. In a locket around his neck, she finds a lock of his mother's grey hair and cries out: "Ich hasse die Philister, hasse Dagon, und hasse mich!"

Much of Act IV is taken up with Samson's life at the mill, where he enters into friendly fellowship with the other slaves and becomes reconciled to his task.

SA-104 (German)

RÖTTGER, KARL. *Simson, Ein Drama.* Leipzig, 1921.

Mi: University of Illinois

Inc.   SAMSON

Mutter, du redest harte Worte—

MIRIAM

Muss ich nicht?

Expl. SAMSON
> Sterbt! Sterbt! Sterbt! Alle, Alle! Gott richtet euch
> noch diesmal und die heilige Flamme meiner
> Empörung.

A PROSE DRAMA of fifty-four pages, without very marked variations from the traditional story.

SA-105 (Russian)

ANDREYEV, LEONID (English translation by HERMAN BERNSTEIN). *Samson in Chains.* New York, 1923

Inc.   SAMSON
> Yahare! Yahare-Orhim! Come here! . . .

Expl.   SAMSON
> Die, my soul, with the Philistines!

IN THIS PROSE DRAMA, Galial, the brother of Delilah, realizes that a mysterious and terrible power works in and through Samson. He therefore seeks to employ it to make himself a king. In the temple of Dagon, Galial and Samson are threatened by the priests and the warriors, but the blind Samson, invoking the supernal power of God, turns them all to stone. Then, feeling that in his blindness he cannot use God's power to increase His glory, he pulls down the temple upon himself and the petrified Philistines.

SA-106 (German)

SALTEN, FELIX. *Simson, Das Schicksal eines Erwählten.*
Zürich, 1928. Mi: Harvard University

Inc.   Er lag flach auf dem Boden, spähte über den Rand der
Grube und lauschte . . .

Expl.   Sie löste den Strick vom Hals, schleuderte ihn weit von
sich, kehrte um und schritt heimwärts.

THIS NARRATIVE PROSE VERSION of the Samson story is full of originality. At the very outset, Samson is laughing over a herd of foxes and jackals that he has captured and penned up in a vault, preparatory to destroying the crops of the Philistines. Delilah is loyal in her love for Samson. The evil genius of the story is her young sister, Kadita, an envious, sex-hungry, and avaricious girl who spies on the pair and overhears Samson's explanation of his strength. She then enters the bedroom while he and Delilah are asleep in each other's arms, cuts off his hair, and delivers him to the Philistines. In the final temple scene, the faithful Delilah stands by him, kisses him, persuades him that he is as strong as ever, and urges him to tear down the pillars so that she may die with him.

SA-107 (French)

LE HARDOUIN, MARIA. *Samson, ou le héros des temps futurs.*
Paris: Corrêa, 1944

Inc. CATINA
Nous allons être en retard. On commence dans cinq minutes et Aglaé n'est pas là! . . .
Expl. SAMSON
Périssent donc ce monde et moi-même pour l'aube d'un jour plus beau.

THIS PLAY DIFFERS so fundamentally from all others on the theme that a summary is in order.

Act I. Samson, after cruel judgment on some Hebrew offenders, withdraws to his tent. One of his guards drags in Delilah who has been caught spying in the neighbourhood. Left alone with her, Samson deliberately reveals to her the secret of his strength because he is weary of invincibility and wants to be like other men. She is at first unwilling to listen; but presently, when he sleeps, she cuts off his long hair and summons the Philistines. Samson, now easily mastered, thanks her. The Philistines put out his eyes.

Act II. Samson, in prison, is mocked by his guards. He becomes aware of nature, in a bird song outside; feels pity for an old blind horse; and becomes aware of himself. The Wandering Jew comes into his cell, and tells him that he can make him aware of a wide range of future experience. Spiritual presences pass before him: Religion, War, Death, and Genius. The first three are repudiated, but self-sacrificing Genius is welcomed as the true secret of life, the faith of the heroes of solitude. Delilah comes and offers to rescue him, but he repulses her.

Act III. An illusionist offers to give him the semblance of his strength. The Wandering Jew, learning that Samson has resolved to die, explains that he has never lost his strength, but only his faith. Delilah again seeks to rescue him, but he refuses to go, and presently, as the guards come in, it is too late. In the final scene of the Act, he is led into the great banqueting scene in the temple of Dagon. He keeps appealing to the banqueters to leave the commonplace, the ordinary, and their god, and face a life of thought and resolute despair. No one hears or understands him. Delilah finally realizes what he intends, is caught by the splendour of his face, and deliberately perishes with him, glorying in his words of pardon. He explains that he is not dying to wreak Jehovah's vengeance on the Philistines but as a servant of mankind, the man of the future, devoted to thought and sacrifice.

Certainly all this is worlds apart from Milton's *Samson Agonistes*. This latest Samson reveals the secret of his strength out of boredom and permanently repudiates Jehovah in favour of intellectual freedom, resolute despair for the individual, and devotion to the future heroes of solitude. Yet the motivation of his final immolation of the Philistines is very vague indeed. He expressly says that he is not killing them as a champion of Jehovah; and it is hard to see why their death has any relevance to his self-destruction as a tribute to future mankind.

Another novelty in the play is the commentary of a chorus of two: Catina and Aglaé. They recite a prologue, and enter again and again as unnoticed commentators, with remarks unheard by the other characters but heard by the audience. They are timeless, as familiar with the future as with the present, and are able to discuss the period of Samson in the light of the twentieth century. Catina is "the spirit of affirmation" and Aglaé "the spirit of negation." Truth is alleged to be half way between them.

Supplement, 1966

SA-88A (Dutch)

VERWEY, ALBERT. *Samson.* Amsterdam, 1896. Available in *Oorspronkelijk Dichtwerk*, 1938, Vol. I, pp. 184–196.

Inc. JONGEN
        Ik ben de voorstad ingelopen, daar ik
        Mijn vader zeggen hoorde dat de Joden-
        Koning, die blind in grinder meelhuis maalt . . .
Expl. JONGEN
        Dat een groot man een goed man doodt, schande is het,
        Schande zo Dagon 't weet.

A DRAMATIC SKETCH of about 375 lines of blank verse. Blind Samson is left sitting in the sun on the festival of Dagon. Five young people (the young son of the commandant of the temple guard, his sweetheart, a smaller boy, a smaller girl and a very little boy) who have heard that he is to play in the temple of Dagon, come and gaze at him. He captures their hearts, holds their small hands in his great hand, and tells them his tragic life-story. He is presently summoned to the temple. The young people gaze from afar, see the catastrophe, and lament the death of Samson and the boy's father—the one a great man and the other a good man.

INDEX OF NAMES